RICH by THIRTY

Lesley-Anne Scorgie

RICH by THIRTY

Your Guide to Financial Success

2ND EDITION

DUNDURN
TORONTO

First edition published in 2007.

Project Editor: Carrie Gleason
Copy Editor: Natalie Meditsky
Printer: Webcom

Cover Design: Laura Boyle
Interior Design: Jesse Hooper
Cover Image: Glen Co Photography

Library and Archives Canada Cataloguing in Publication

Scorgie, Lesley, author
    Rich by thirty : your guide to financial success / Lesley-Anne Scorgie.

Issued in print and electronic formats.
Includes index.
Originally published as: Rich by thirty : a young adult's guide to financial success, 2007.
ISBN 978-1-4597-2974-2 (pbk.).--ISBN 978-1-4597-2975-9 (pdf).--
ISBN 978-1-4597-2976-6 (epub)

    1. Young adults--Finance, Personal. 2. Teenagers--Finance, Personal. 3. Financial literacy. I. Title.

HG179.S353 2015   332.0240084'2   C2014-907391-7
                                                 C2014-907392-5

1   2   3   4   5   19   18   17   16   15

We acknowledge the support of the **Canada Council for the Arts** and the **Ontario Arts Council** for our publishing program. We also acknowledge the financial support of the **Government of Canada** through the **Canada Book Fund** and **Livres Canada Books,** and the **Government of Ontario** through the **Ontario Book Publishing Tax Credit** and the **Ontario Media Development Corporation.**

Care has been taken to trace the ownership of copyright material used in this book. The author and the publisher welcome any information enabling them to rectify any references or credits in subsequent editions.

J. Kirk Howard, President

The publisher is not responsible for websites or their content unless they are owned by the publisher.

Printed and bound in Canada.

VISIT US AT
Dundurn.com | *@dundurnpress* | *Facebook.com/dundurnpress* | *Pinterest.com/Dundurnpress*

Dundurn
3 Church Street, Suite 500
Toronto, Ontario, Canada
M5E 1M2

To my Grandmother Scorgie. Words cannot express how much your love, care, and influence have meant to me through the years. You are the greatest woman I have ever met — full of strength, courage, intelligence, beauty, and support. I am so blessed to have you in my life.

Contents

Introduction

You are young. You are smart. You are stylish. But, like the majority of under-30s, you are feeling really freakin' broke.

Tired of stressing out to pay for groceries, let alone your future?

Reading *Rich by Thirty* is the first step toward creating an awesome and "rich" future for yourself. And, no — you won't have to eat instant noodles or skip regular bathing for the next decade to achieve your goals.

For our generation, "rich" isn't just about money. These days, we're looking for balance and personal fulfillment, too. We seek opportunities for growth, flexibility, and fun in our working and personal lives. And we're well aware that money doesn't necessarily provide all of the above.

On the one hand, I think it is fantastic that our generation is willing to separate the pursuit of happiness from that of monetary success. On the other, I truly believe that not caring about money is a big mistake! Being smart about your money — how you spend it and how you manage it — can make a huge difference to the quality of your life. It can open doors or close them. It can help you realize your goals and dreams, or ensure that you won't.

Becoming "rich by 30" requires us to strike a balance between our financial, personal, and career growth. That's right — it's not just about our finances. When these three areas are strong, we can reach our full potential.

Think of it like this. If you're entirely focused on your job but neglect your friends and family in the process, you may achieve your career goals at the expense of your personal relationships — #LonelyAtTheTop. On the flip side, if you pay zero attention to your finances, you'll have no money to afford the things in life that you're striving for, like travel or a home purchase — #DreamsCostMoney. Or consider how powerful healthy personal relationships can be for your career and finances — #SupportPays.

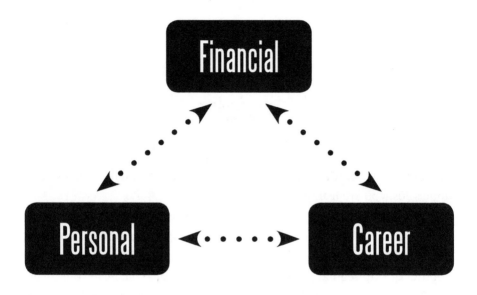

Rich by Thirty will give you practical advice to strengthen your financial, personal, and career skills so that you can build up your bank account quickly and be happy in the process.

WHY LISTEN TO ME?

Before you read any further, you'd probably like to know a little more about me. Who am I, and why am I telling you how to manage your money? Good questions!

I was born in Toronto into an average family. My mom stayed at home until I was four years old and my dad worked as a paramedic. When I was eight, my family moved out west to Edmonton so that both of my parents could go back to school and upgrade their educations. As you can imagine, with my parents in school, money was *very* tight. When they graduated in 1998, my family moved again — this time to Calgary, so that my parents could look for work in their respective fields. Unfortunately, finding and keeping jobs was difficult for my parents and so for many years after that my family continued to struggle financially.

I didn't grow up in a wealthy home. Far from it. For most of my pre-teen and teenage years, my family survived on $24,000 a year. That managed to feed and clothe five people, pay a small mortgage, pay my parents' tuition, and maintain one vehicle. We had very small Christmas gifts, generic-brand food, and no lavish vacations. My brother, sister, and I relied on second-hand stores for our bicycles, clothing, and toys. There was no money to spare. It was during that time that I learned to live a frugal and fun life. That meant my entire family would look for deals, sales, and giveaways while still finding affordable ways to enjoy our lives. We never paid full price for anything!

It's not hard to figure out that my interest in money was sparked by the lack of it in my own home. Even at an early age, I'd carry around my piggy bank and inquire about the different coins I'd collected and what I could purchase with them. My parents kindly answered most of my money questions, even though they were drowning in debt and bills. They also encouraged me to read up on my interest. Soon I began flipping through *Forbes* magazine, *The Economist*, and *Report on Business*. I picked my way through various articles and understood at least some of what I read. While I was reading about stock picking and entrepreneurial endeavours, my best friends were watching fun shows and getting into computers. I joined them on occasion, but more times than not, I fell deeper into my own interests.

As early as eight, I was operating a lemonade stand during the summer months and shovelling snow during the winter. I wanted to earn enough money for a trip to the pool, a visit to the candy store, or an outing to a movie. I set my sights, knew my targets, and went for it. As time passed, my initial motivations for saving and investing evolved from "making enough to go to the movies" to "making enough to retire with millions."

On my tenth birthday I received $100 in cash and bought my first Canada Savings Bond. My mother helped me understand that by making an investment of $100 then, it would be worth $135 seven years down the road. When I realized I could earn "free" money on my small investment, I took every chance I got to buy more bonds using my birthday and holiday money, as well as cash from my flyer route and babysitting.

When I turned 14, I started working at the local public library. Not only did the job earn me a small income, the books and newspapers I found on the shelves gave me the chance to learn more about growing money. I took it upon myself to investigate options for investing my money. I bought my first mutual funds that same year and began investing in the stock market four years later, when I was 18. Once I started to see the growth in my own accounts — the power of compounded interest and reinvested returns — I was hooked!

FROM FRUGAL TO EXTRAORDINARY: THE OPRAH EXPERIENCE

In grade 12 my management and marketing class was learning about investing. My teacher was having difficulty explaining the concept to our class because my peers were totally unresponsive. One day, in complete frustration, she asked if any student would like to try teaching this part of the course. I raised my hand and away we went.

I taught a few classes and shared my money knowledge with my friends. It just so happened that, during the same week, a local newspaper randomly phoned the school to ask if there were any "odd or interesting" students they could profile. I was nominated due to my financial knowledge. The newspaper agreed that I fit the criteria — I hoped I was more interesting than odd! — and they went ahead with the interview. They published a front-page article entitled "Whiz Kid" and then posted it on the Internet.

In February 2001 I received a phone call from a producer at the *Oprah Winfrey Show*. She had seen the article on the Internet and wanted to talk about my investment and money management savvy. Two weeks later, I was on the show!

The theme was "Ordinary People, Extraordinary Wealth." I was one of a few guests who were sharing their financial savvy and secrets with more than 20 million viewers! What set me apart from the others? I was the only guest under the age of 40 *and* I'd managed to save a sizeable sum — more than even my parents. I was there to demonstrate that you can have a very typical young life and still make positive financial choices.

Since being on *Oprah*, I have completed my bachelor of commerce degree and masters of business administration and written for a number of newspapers and magazines. I own a house and have an awesome partner. I'm an entrepreneur and started an online money school called MeVest, and I have savings for the future. I also have a lot of fun! By the time I retire, I'll have millions of dollars. Because of this success, I've become a spokesperson and advocate for young people who want to chase their dreams and be fully equipped to handle the price tag. My passion is for teaching and speaking about money management and financial literacy. I have delivered presentations to thousands of people across North America, with audiences ranging in age from 6 to 80.

Before we go any further, I want to assure you that I was (and still am!) *normal* — like you! I went to school, worked a part-time job through high school and university, and completed my homework even when it was tough or boring. When I graduated, I got a full-time job and worked hard at that, too. I travelled. I bought a car. I purchased a home. On weekends, I socialized with friends and squeezed in a little relaxing time. I went through the same ups and downs that every young person experiences. The only difference? I wanted to be wealthy by the time I was 30 and I started planning earlier than usual to make that happen.

Today, at 30, I am rich and I did it myself. And the best part is that I haven't had to make huge sacrifices to get there.

Now I want to show you how you can become rich by 30 too.

LISTEN UP!

Out of all the advice you'll read in the pages that follow, this could be the most important: you can do extraordinary things with your life. You may think that you can't, or that what little money you have to contribute to your own financial future isn't enough. You can, and it is. All of your time, talent, money, and effort will pay off in the long run — literally and figuratively — if you can focus on making positive financial choices today.

So how do you do it? This book is going to get you started. As you read, you will find useful information on getting motivated and organized, pursuing your education, getting smart with your money, and getting started with your career, savings, and investing. Perhaps for the first time in your life, you'll be getting financial advice from someone your own age — someone like you. You'll learn about basic money management, including how to make or find money, debt reduction, budgeting, getting a job, and investment strategies. You'll learn how to live a frugal life without making painstaking sacrifices. You'll learn why it makes so much sense to start planning when you're young, and why it pays to diversify. You'll learn tips and tricks to pay for college, university, trade, or technical school. You'll learn the difference between savings and investments, and pick up some short- and long-term investing strategies. Perhaps most importantly, you'll learn that money is only one part of a balanced and happy life — personal and career satisfaction are just as important.

When the tips, techniques, and strategies on the pages that follow are combined, they make for a very "rich" lifestyle and great personal and financial fulfillment. This book doesn't offer a "get rich quick" scheme. It is about learning the financial fundamentals that will secure your financial future in the long term. And by reading it, you are well on your way to financial success.

Happy saving!

CHAPTER 1
Get Motivated: Why Money Matters

A FEW BORING TRUTHS

Ready or not, the future is upon you. Before you even know it, you'll be thinking about things like the cost of college, mortgages, cars, kids, vacations, and — yup — retirement! It may sound boring, but it's your responsibility to think about these things. You must take positive steps now so that you can create the future you want. You are the only one who can make your dreams — financial and otherwise — come true. If you don't look out for your future, who will?

The Sort-of-Boring Truth about the Distant Future

Kevin is 23 years old and the youngest of three children in his family. His mom and dad are both in their mid-60s, but neither can afford to retire. The situation is starting to worry Kevin. His parents seem tired all the time, and he's concerned about their health. He's even started to take on extra shifts at work, in between classes at school, so he can help out with the bills and groceries. One thing Kevin knows for sure is that he doesn't want to end up in the same position when he turns 60! He knows the only way to avoid this scenario is to work hard now and get smart with his money.

Money is the key to your long-term financial security. It's scary to think about this, but by the time you're ready to retire, you will need approximately four times the amount of money that you need now — just to live the way you're living now (keep those "lifestyles of the rich and famous" fantasies in check!). This hard-to-swallow truth is due to a nasty little thing called **inflation**. Inflation makes the dollars in your bank account today less powerful as time goes by. For example, four dollars today might be worth only one dollar 40 years from now.

Think about it this way: A 65-year-old woman with $1 million in retirement savings could call it quits tomorrow and not have to live below the poverty line. However, 40 years from now, a 65-year-old woman wanting to call it quits would need to have socked away $4 million to maintain her lifestyle! Another way to look at it? One million dollars today will be worth only $250,000 in 40 years. This is what financial gurus refer to as the time value of money, which essentially means that money is worth more today than in the future.

If this isn't scary or depressing enough, wait until you hear the next part! The next time you receive a paycheque, have a look at the section on the stub where the deductions are listed. There are deductions for income tax and government pension plans, like Canada's Canada Pension Plan (CPP) or Social Security in the United States. There may even be deductions for things like medical and employment/unemployment insurance. On average, for every dollar you earn, you're really taking home only 65 to 70 cents, and sometimes less. What it boils down to is that the taxman and government get paid before anyone else, including you — the one who earned the paycheque in the first place.

Think the government's retirement savings plan will be enough for you? Think again. The government's retirement savings program will help you to a small degree. But that money will not allow you to retire comfortably because it's a small sum. We'll more than likely have to count on ourselves to assure our financial security.

Boring, and a little bit depressing, but true.

So your money becomes less powerful and less valuable as time passes. And you're not likely to get much help from the government, or anyone else, for that matter. Are you ever going to be able to retire? Or buy a house? Or go to college? Or have a wedding? Or go on vacation? Of course you will — if you learn to care about your money. Handled properly and managed wisely, your money can not only keep up with inflation, it can beat it!

The Not-So-Boring Truth about the Not-So-Distant Future

Maya is 16 years old and in her second-last year of high school. She has average grades and comes from a financially average household. She loves to hang out with her friends, dance, and, most importantly, shop. Recently Maya has started to think about what she might want to do with her life. She made an appointment with the guidance counsellor at school to discuss her dream of becoming a children's doctor. When she sat down with the counsellor, however, she discovered two things: the cost of medical school was very high and her grades would also have to be very high for her to have any chance of getting a scholarship.

Now Maya's reconsidering. Unless something changes — both with her commitment to school and her financial planning — her dream will never become a reality.

If you were drifting off during the last section — or at least wondering why you need to think about retirement when you're still in your teens or twenties — maybe this section will hit home a little harder. You need to care about your money because, even though you're young, money still affects you. In fact, money affects everyone.

What do you want to do with your life? Do you want to be a pilot? A nurse? A musician? You'll need money to do it. Money is also necessary if you want to go snowboarding, buy a house, travel, or shop.

It comes down to this: money enables us to have choices. The more we understand about it — how to make it, how to save and invest it, how to spend it wisely — the more freedom we'll have. Think about how dull your life would be if you didn't have enough money to go to a movie with a friend. Think about how frustrated you would be if you really wanted to become a doctor, like Maya, but couldn't afford the tuition fees. The more financial freedom you have, the more freedom you'll have in all areas of your life, including in your career and personal life. You'll be free to make the choices that best suit your needs and goals. And isn't that what everyone wants?

THE $5,000 QUESTION

If you came home and found a cheque for $5,000 in your mailbox, what would you do with it? Would you save the money or buy a car, some clothes, or a hot new sound system? Would you give some to charity, pay off a loan, or take your friends out for a fabulous dinner? Would you start a business? It's nice to have so many options, isn't it?

Now consider the opposite situation. Your most recent shopping trip got a little out of hand and you're looking at a $5,000 credit card bill! What are your options now? You either pay it back or the bank will repossess your car! Remember, money leads to choices, and choices lead to freedom.

Now Matters

Tony is 29 years old and was shifting nervously in a chair across from the loan officer at his local bank. He held his breath as the bank issued its verdict: *yes*. Based on the strength of his business plan and good credit history, they had agreed to give him a small loan to cover the costs for some electricians' equipment. Now his plans to start his own residential electrician company would come true!

What you choose to do with your money today matters because it can impact your decisions in the future. In Tony's case, if he hadn't been responsible with his money in prior years, his credit score would have been weak and he wouldn't have qualified for his small business loan.

The Not-So-Boring Truth about Time

I know, I know. All this stuff about retirement and choices and freedom makes perfect sense to you, but still…. You're probably scratching your head right now, trying to figure out how you — an average person under 30 with hardly any disposable income (the income you have left over after your bills are paid) — are supposed to take control of your financial life when some 50- and 60-year-olds haven't gotten the hang of it yet. They have good jobs, and houses, and lots of other stuff that you don't, right? That's true. But you've got one thing that they don't have, and it may be the most important thing of all: time.

Time is a pretty handy thing to have on your side. With time, you can grow your money substantially without doing nearly as much work as you might expect. You can do this through the power of **compounded interest and reinvested returns**.

Imagine yourself at the top of a hill, making a snowball. It's a nice, round snowball that takes you all of 30 seconds to make. When you aren't looking, the wind blows the snowball down the hill. As it's rolling, it picks up more and more snow until, a couple of minutes later and with no additional help from you, a giant snowball stops at the bottom of the hill. That's how compounded interest and reinvested returns works. You earn interest on your initial investment, which is then reinvested, allowing you to earn interest on that as well. So now you're earning interest on the interest on your original investment. As time passes, your money grows, like the rolling snowball, into something quite impressive.

The table below is an abbreviated version of one you'll see later, in chapter 7. For now, all you need to know is that if you start early enough and contribute to an investment plan regularly, you can turn yourself into a self-made millionaire. In this example, a young person starts saving $100 per month until the age of 65 and retires a millionaire! (This example assumes a 9 percent annualized rate of return and rounds to the nearest $100.)

COMPOUND INTEREST

Age	Saved per month ($)	Total saved ($)*
15	100	1,300
25	100	23,000
35	100	74,200
45	100	195,600
55	100	483,000
65	100	1,163,400

*With compounded interest and reinvested returns.

Impressive, isn't it? With only $100 per month you can become a millionaire! Wondering where the heck you'll find $100 per month to contribute to an investment account? Read on! *Rich by Thirty* will show you how to live frugally without foregoing fun, and how to make more dough so you can afford your savings contributions.

Now, think about how much more money you would have if you increased your monthly contributions as you advance in your life and career — you'd achieve millionaire status much faster!

If the table isn't enough to inspire you, think about it this way: you can actually double, triple, and quadruple your money with the power of compounded interest and reinvested returns. I'd like to introduce you to what investment types call the **Rule of 72**. Basically, it helps you figure out how long, based on a fixed interest rate, it will take for your money to double.

This is how it the formula works:

Time it will take for your money to double = 72 / rate of return

So, if you keep your money in a growth-oriented portfolio (more on that in chapter 8) that is averaging a 12 percent rate of return, it will take six years for your money to double (72 / 12 = 6). On the other hand, if your ordinary savings account is earning 2 percent, you're looking at 36 years to double your money! See what a difference your rate of return can make?

MAKING IT PERSONAL

I'm hoping that by now you've developed a greater appreciation of what money can do for you — how you can make it work to your advantage, how it can change your life for the better. I'm also hoping that you're sufficiently motivated to dive in and get started. It's never too early (or too late) to take control of your financial future.

Goals Lead and Dreams Follow

Do you have dreams and goals? Of course you do. Have you ever wanted something so badly that you simply had to find a way to get it?

Throughout my university years, I dreamed about having my own place when I graduated. For four years I saved a little money each month so that I'd have enough for a small down payment on a townhome upon graduation. My *goal* of owning a place led me to take *actions* that would make it happen. Now my *dream* of owning a home has come true.

Goals → Actions → Dreams

Goals don't have to be huge to be real. Your goal could be to buy a bike next year. Or you may want to complete your full education with no student debt. Perhaps you want to save enough money to start up your own tech company. To set goals, you must look into your future and figure out where you want to go and what you want to do and have.

This goal business can be tricky. Some goals, like saving for a computer or a car, make perfect sense. Others, like winning the lottery and retiring to Hawaii, may not be so practical. When you set your goals, there are a few things you can do to make sure they have a real chance of happening.

- **Think short and long term:** Sometimes it can take years to have a clear idea of where you want to go, especially when it comes to your money. What do you see for yourself in the future? Does travel, a car, a wedding, a boat, a business, or a house fit into your plans? Do you have specific savings goals, like saving a million dollars by age 40? Jot down some of your high-level goals and dreams below.

My Goals and Dreams

- _____
- _____
- _____
- _____

Do you notice anything in common among your goals? That's right — they all cost money! Head back up to your list and put a price tag beside each. No, you don't need to be exact. Just be realistic. If you're unsure what owning a Ferrari or having a child will cost, a quick Google search will reveal the answer. You need a plan in order to afford your goals. That's where SMART goals can help.

- **Create SMART goals:** SMART goals are **S**pecific, **M**easurable, **A**ttainable, **R**ealistic, and **T**imely. Rather than writing down a goal that states, "I want to be a millionaire," you might try this: "I want to have $1 million by the time I'm 65, using the financial fundamentals and investing techniques I have learned in *Rich by Thirty*." That goal is much clearer than the first and it has all the elements of a SMART goal.

    - **Specific:** Provide specific details about your goal and why you're working toward it.
    - **Measurable:** How will you measure if you're successful?
    - **Attainable:** How do you plan to achieve your goal?
    - **Realistic:** Does your goal and the plan you have to achieve it seem realistic?
    - **Timely:** When will you achieve your goal?

Take a moment to revisit and revise the goals and dreams you wrote down previously to make them SMART.

MY SMART GOALS

High-level goal	Specific	Measurable	Attainable	Realistic	Timely

- **Write your SMART goals down:** Committing your goals to paper is like developing a contract with yourself — one that only you can accomplish or break. People who write down their goals are more likely to achieve them than people who do not. You may want to keep your goals close to you, perhaps stuck to your refrigerator, so that you are constantly reminded of what you're working toward.

- **Create a personal vision statement:** Writing a personal vision statement is a huge step toward financial, personal, and career success. A vision statement is somewhat aspirational in that it helps you set your sights on something huge that you want to work toward over a long period of time. It is a mental picture of what you want to achieve over a time period of five to ten years. A good vision statement will include the following:

  - **Who** (you!)
  - **What** (the goal)
  - **When** (the time frame)
  - **How** (the action plan)

Here is an example of a personal vision statement to support that goal:

> I, Jane Smith, want to be free from financial and career worries so that I can be happy and can focus on my personal relationships. Thus, I will work toward achieving financial success by retirement by using tired-and-true financial fundamentals including spending wisely, making more money, saving and investing, and giving back to the community.

My personal vision statement is:

> I, Lesley-Anne Scorgie, want to be happy and satisfied financially, personally, and professionally. I want to grow

my relationships and my bank account while having a positive impact on people by inspiring them to reach their potential through my books, public speaking, and my business, MeVest.

Writing your personal vision statement can be a lot of fun. But, sometimes it's difficult to know where we really want to go in the long term. Most of us, though, have at least some sort of idea. So give it a whirl below, and don't worry if it takes a couple of tries to get it right.

———————————————————————————————

———————————————————————————————

———————————————————————————————

———————————————————————————————

———————————————————————————————

You may want to design your vision statement as a certificate, print it off, and frame it. Hang it on your wall so that whenever you see it, you are reminded of the positive direction in which you are headed.

I use my personal vision statement as a reminder of what I want to do with my life. But as time passes and I change, so do my goals and sometimes even my vision. Don't feel too boxed in by one statement or one set of goals. Make changes to your vision as it becomes clearer over time.

EXCUSES, EXCUSES!

What's holding you back? Make a list of all the reasons you don't think you can get your finances in order. Then put it somewhere safe and prepare to tear it up in the not-too-distant future. Once you get through the next several chapters you won't need it anymore because you'll be on your way. Nothing will hold you back!

Hopefully, you're feeling a little more inspired and motivated than you were when you started reading a few pages back. You know how important it is to start working on your financial future as early as possible, and you know how integral money can be to your future — both short and long term. Now you're ready to put the wheels in motion. You're ready to go out and make it happen!

CHAPTER 2
Get Educated: The Payoff for Hitting the Books

I know, I know. Studying is no fun! But your efforts at school will pay off in a major way. In the long run, educated people earn WAY more money and have a far better quality of life than those without formal education. Though it may feel super painful to pay for your schooling and work tirelessly on your courses, it's well worth your efforts.

THE TEMPTATION

Joseph, 18 years old, had worked at his uncle's oil-field services company for three summers in a row, cleaning and learning to maintain equipment. Because he continued to live with his parents and had limited expenses throughout those years, he'd managed to save a whopping $10,000. Upon graduating high school, Joseph's uncle offered him a full-time job with an annual salary of $50,000. *Wowie!* Joseph thought. Not only was that a lot of money, but he could avoid the costs of paying hefty tuition bills by choosing to work full time rather than going to university. Visions of houses, snowmobiles, and cars started dancing through his head. But his parents strongly encouraged him to follow his original plans to go to university to become a mechanical engineer. He agreed to weigh the pros and cons of both options.

Have you ever wondered how much it really costs to go to school?

The average cost for a four-year university, college, trade, or technical program ranges between $20,000 and $50,000 — and that doesn't include living expenses or purchasing a computer, textbooks, and software. But it doesn't end there. Because you are in school, you give up the opportunity to work full time and make some money. Let's say you could count on an annual salary of $30,000 if you didn't go to school. Over the course of your four-year program, you'd be "losing" a potential $120,000 in income. Add that to the $20,000 to $50,000 in tuition expenses PLUS the amount you'll spend on books and technology, and your post-secondary education is "costing" you well over $140,000!

Are you asking yourself why you should bother making an investment in college, university, trade school, technical school, or other post-secondary education? Considering that 75 percent of future jobs will require education past high school, the answer is *yes*![1] Certainly, there are very successful people in North America without higher education. But this phenomenon is becoming less common because the corporate cultural norm has changed: education is critical.

Of all the investments out there, which you'll learn about throughout *Rich by Thirty*, education is the safest and most lucrative investment you can make.

From a "safe" perspective, education is something that can never be taken away from you. And regardless of what you study in school, your education will broaden your way of thinking, expand your skill set, and make you far more competitive in the workforce. Education can also, in some instances, save you from the labour intensity of many jobs that don't require an education. This may not seem like a big deal now, but a tired and/or weak body in the future will inhibit your ability to continue working comfortably in a job that requires physical labour.

Financially speaking, according to the National Graduate's Survey (Statistics Canada) and a 2013 report from the U.S. Census Bureau entitled "The Big Payoff," when you invest in *any* type of education past high school, your long-term income-earning ability is a few hundred thousand dollars to over a million dollars greater than a high school graduate's.[2,3] So, though the short-term pains of student loans may seem unbearable, it's worth the long-term gains in income throughout your working career.

Research has also shown that educated young people not only earn more money, they also enjoy a higher quality of life because they have more choices in terms of career opportunities and lifestyle.

Back to Joseph for a moment. If he succumbs to the temptation of a seemingly high income now, he will forego the much higher income the mechanical engineering route would have provided him later in life. Plus, his risk of injury in a manual labour job is much higher. In addition to that, he'd miss out on the opportunity to grow his skill set, broaden his thinking, and experience the social connections and friendships that a higher education often provides.

So, if you're on the fence about formal education, like Joseph is, weigh your list of pros and cons regarding your future job security, income, skills, and quality of life.

IT STARTS EARLY

Preparing for and investing in your education should start early and well before your last year of high school. If you haven't already spoken to your parents about the cost of your future education, ask if they have money set aside for it. If they do, great! Find out how much, to determine if it's enough. If they don't, you'll need to start saving up or brace yourself to take on student debt.

When I was about 13 years old, my parents sat me down and told me that they would not be able to help me pay for university because they simply didn't have the savings. Thankfully, my grandmother had set aside some money to help pay my way, but the majority of the costs for my program, living expenses, and supplies would have to be paid by me. It didn't take me very long to kick into savings "high gear." I babysat as often as I could and got a job at the local library at age 14. Whatever I earned, I saved at least half, if not a little more.

Wondering how you can start saving up for school? In chapter 6 you'll learn how.

Working hard to achieve your best marks and top performance in extracurricular activities will also help you compete for awards, scholarships, and bursaries, which can be worth thousands of FREE dollars. And great marks combined with volunteer efforts, sports, or musical training will help support your application to whatever educational program you choose to apply for. When you're finally accepted into your post-secondary program, you can apply for additional awards, grants, bursaries, and more through your campus registrar's office or library.

It's School, Not a Fashion Show

Feeling stressed about back-to-school shopping? You're not alone! According to a survey conducted by Visa, North Americans feel frazzled by the crowds and gouged at the till for books, school supplies, and back-to-school paraphernalia.[4]

Save money on back-to-school shopping by slicing your budget in half, starting early, and getting creatively frugal.

Before hitting the shopping centre, take inventory of what you already have: pens, paper, notebooks, binders, computer, software, backpacks, et cetera. Don't buy new supplies just because you want them. This is financially unwise and environmentally wasteful. You can also shop for necessary supplies throughout the year when stores have sales. Many stores will blow out inventory at clearance prices throughout the year to stimulate sales volumes. Get there early before the quality supplies have been picked over.

Hit up thrift shops, garage sales, neighbourhood clothing exchanges, and websites like eBay or Craigslist. See if you can pick up gently used supplies, computers, furniture, or clothing. Stores like Costco and other wholesalers carry a wide variety of back-to-school inventory at affordable prices. If you've outgrown clothes or no longer need old textbooks, sell them on consignment or exchange them with friends.

Though it's convenient to buy lunches, try to avoid doing so. Plan packed lunches for yourself while at school. You'll save loads of money and can ensure your meals are nutritious.

You don't need to spend hundreds of dollars on back-to-school shopping. School is a place of learning, not a fashion show. Focus on purchasing essential items.

Start Working. Start Budgeting. Start Filing Taxes.

Besides saving up in advance for school, if you're struggling to cover your tuition tab, get a job.

Apply for a paid co-op, internship, or a work-experience program related to your field of study. These opportunities are posted on employer and career-centre websites. Aim for full-time work in the summer and a part-time arrangement while you're in school.

If this doesn't appeal to you, spice it up with an overseas work term. When my brother finished his first year of college he applied to an online request for English teachers in China. He vetted the hiring institution through the college he attended, arranged a Skype interview, and won the competition for the position. He spent the next eight months working abroad, travelling and experiencing a new culture. Guidance counselling or career offices at your school will post opportunities for overseas work terms on their online job board. You can also check out online international job boards through a quick Google search. If you find a nifty opportunity, get a reference or two about the organization to ensure it's a legitimate employer, prior to jetting off. Be aware that most international employers will not pay for your flight or accommodation (at least in the long term), so you'll need to work that into your budget.

While classes are in session, work on or near campus. Your faculty, libraries, restaurants, stores, and fitness centres all need staff. If you're feeling entrepreneurial, turn your hobbies into money: photography, writing, web design, et cetera.

Student debt is often unavoidable. But by working throughout and saving up your income, you can significantly offset the costs of tuition. This will give you greater financial flexibility after graduation. Plus, working is a great way to meet friends and grow your professional experience. Whatever you do, ensure you've got sufficient time to focus on your studies.

Draw up a budget the moment you've settled into your new routine. Using a spreadsheet or online banking budget-tracking tool, list income and expenses (big and small). Apply "financial bootstrapping" techniques to live financially lean and frugal: reduce cell phone bills and dinners out; live with family if it is geographically feasible, if not, live off campus with roommates; and negotiate for better rental rates or move to a smaller and cheaper place. Buy textbooks, laptops, desks, and furniture second-hand. (There are more budget tips in chapter 4.)

You should also file a tax return. Even though you're not making significant income, by filing a tax return you'll be entitled to receive government credits, which can amount to hundreds of dollars in cash every year. Plus, you can claim valuable tuition credits. Unused credits can be carried forward into the future when you'll be earning more income. In certain circumstances, moving expenses can be claimed, along with credits for using public transportation. If you're using student loans, you can claim federal and provincial tax credits for the interest you pay throughout the year. Use the free tax services offered by your school to ensure you're benefiting from all the credits and deductions available to you.

WHAT EVERY STUDENT SHOULD KNOW BEFORE SIGNING A LEASE

The countdown is on: you're about to fly the nest! It'll be just you, your roommates, books, essays, late-night study sessions, and maybe the odd party (okay, make that *lots* of parties). But what about that all-important roof over your head?

You need a game plan when it comes to your pad. Before you commit to forking over cash on the first cool place you see, ask yourself these questions:

- **Budget:** What's your budget? If you don't know how to budget, we're going to show you in a few short chapters. You know better than anyone what your cash flow can handle each month, so stay within it. Otherwise you'll add a layer of distracting financial stress to your already full school schedule.

- **Location:** Is the place close enough to school, the grocery store, and other amenities so you can keep your commuting time and costs to a minimum? Is public transit nearby? If not, do you save enough money by living further away that it outweighs these costs?

- **Roommates:** Have you found the right roommates? No, this isn't just about saving money on rent and utilities. It's about ensuring your personalities are compatible. If not, you'll spend way too much time worrying about the things that irritate you, like dirty dishes and smelly clothes, and not nearly enough energy on your studies. You'll also want to make sure the people you live with know the importance of paying their share of the rent on time — you don't want to be on the hook for covering for them. Hash out these tough issues *before* you decide to become roomies.

- **Legal Responsibility:** If you're dabbling in the roommate realm, you'll need to determine who will ultimately sign the lease and take legal responsibility for the place. If it's possible, have all the roommates listed on the lease. Some landlords will ask to look up your credit score to see if you're a safe bet for paying your rent on time. Many students don't have much in the way of credit and may need a parent to co-sign a lease. Talk about this possibility with your folks ahead of time.

If you've done your research and you're ready to rent, here are some practical considerations, most of which are negotiable with your landlord:

- **Cost:** The cost of the rent and what it includes. If utilities, laundry, and parking are extra, work that into your budget and clearly state it in your lease. Don't get sideswiped with add-ons you didn't agree to.

- **Term:** Are you getting into a month-to-month, full year, or lease term that lasts only for the school year? Most landlords push for a year, but many allow students to rent only for the months they're in school.

- **Damage Deposit:** Are you prepared for the amount and conditions of the damage deposit? How does your landlord plan to reconcile the condition of your place before and after you lease it out? It can help to take plenty of before and after pictures to establish your position if there ends up being a disagreement upon your departure.

- **Notice:** Can your landlord kick you out with 60 days notice? That would be an issue if you were in the middle of exams. Consider the opposite situation where you need to break the lease. What are the penalties for doing so?

- **Eviction:** What will it take to get evicted? Not paying the rent? Loud noise? Drug use? Vandalizing the property? You need to find out. Generally speaking, if you treat the property as your own, practice common courtesy, and pay rent on time and in full, you shouldn't have issues.

- **Repairs:** Who will be responsible for which repairs? How will you notify your landlord of issues? It's very common for tenants to be responsible for repairs under $50, such as replacing light bulbs.

- **Community Rules:** In many cases, condominiums and apartments have common property and strict rules around how that property is to be used. You should review these rules, determine how they will affect you, and ask your landlord if there is a need to "sign off" on them prior to signing the lease.

- **Changes to the Property:** Are you allowed to paint, hang art, copy keys, and swap out the furniture? This may be important as you're establishing your much-needed Zen for school.

- **Read:** Don't skim your lease agreement! The devil is always in the details. Take it home for a thorough review and consult with your student resource centre if you have questions. You might also want to understand the basic legal rights between tenants and landlords in your province or city. A quick Google search can provide this information.

WELL PAST HIGH SCHOOL? YOU'RE NOT ALONE

Jodi was contemplating whether to head back to school after working for four years as a legal assistant. At the age of 25, she was thinking she was too old to join the ranks of so many others studying. But the income she would earn as a legal business analyst versus a legal assistant would be nearly 70 percent greater. But the cost to Jodi would be three years of additional schooling.

Many people choose to go back to school after they've been working for many years and already have financial commitments, such as a mortgage, rent, or car payments. My parents did it while I was growing up in the hopes of increasing their collective income and creating a better life for our family. The costs, however, were very inhibitive for our family and essentially pushed us below the poverty line for nearly a decade because they had to forego much of their income-earning capacity in exchange for their education. Ultimately it was worth it because they did make more money, but our budget was very lean and sacrifices were made during that time.

If you're thinking of heading back to school later in life or your career, go for it! But be smart about it so you can avoid financial hardship in the process. There are two ways to balance the commitment — part time or full time.

My pal Maria does the part-time school route. She is a young mother of three children, and between working 40 hours a week and shuttling her children between dance lessons and karate practice, she has time to take only one night class each semester as she works to complete a bachelor of arts degree at her local university. Sure, it will take her almost five times as long to complete her degree as it would if she were a full-time student, but having balance between her schooling, work, and personal life is important to her.

My other pal Angela took a year off to complete her masters of business administration (MBA) full time. For Angela, this meant forgoing her healthy income as a geologist for 12 months in exchange for completing her master's program much faster. But the moment she graduated, her income bumped up 40 percent, which helped to offset the costs of forgoing it for a year.

In either scenario, you'll be able to achieve a higher level of education. The biggest consideration for you will be whether to forgo your current income in order to expedite the process. If you have a partner or children, going to school full-time might not work well for you and your budget. Whereas if you're single and living on your own, the only person you'll be affecting financially, and with your lack of availability, is you.

INFORMAL EDUCATION

Education can also be informal. Take, for example, Jack, a young fitness trainer. He'd like to broaden his fitness expertise into teaching spin classes. In order to learn how to do this, he doesn't need to take a formal class, he just needs to learn the skills from an expert spin instructor.

Think about where you'd like to take your career in the next 5 to 10 years. What types of skills and education will you need to make your career goals a reality? If you're not sure, speak to someone who has the type of job you'd like to have. For example, if you'd like to become the site manager of the construction site you currently work on, spend time with the current foreperson. Inquire about education, accreditations, and specific skill sets. Ask for some specific advice on what you could do in terms of education and skills to advance your career. If you don't have those kinds of connections, reviewing job postings for your dream job can be equally beneficial. The postings should clearly state the skills, experience, and education required for the role.

When you have a clear idea of where you want to take your career, you can determine the appropriate level of investment in your own education and skills. Whether you hit the books or not, develop skills that will give you a competitive edge and make you difficult to replace. Competitive skill sets provide leverage during salary negotiations and greater options for advancement and promotion.

CAN EDUCATION BE A BAD INVESTMENT?

There are two ways in which education can be a bad investment. The first is if you overdo it with student loans and lines of credit, meaning you get more than what you need in order to have extra spending money or make car payments. This will thrust you into unnecessary debt, which is very hard to pay off upon graduation.

The second is if you choose a program with limited employment opportunities available in that field. This would force you into a situation where you are required to complete additional, and more practical, education or face unemployment or a lower salary after graduating. Yes, you still need to be true to yourself and what you want to study, but blend that with practical skills. So if, for example, you're doing a fine arts major, you may also want to take classes on bookkeeping so you could potentially get a job managing an art shop while still enjoying the beauty of art.

Practical skills are vital and you often get those through a combination of courses and working experiences. So do your best to blend these together. Ultimately, though, getting an education will always pay off in that it will broaden your thinking, which can then be applied to whatever you put your mind to.

CHAPTER 3
Get Organized: File Folders, Banks, and You

Organization truly *is* the key to success. In fact, on the road to wealth and splendour, getting organized is the most important step to take. This process is often referred to as "getting your financial house in order." It may sound a little intimidating, but it's not. It can actually be fun.

THE TOOLS OF THE TRADE

Meet Erica, age 26. She works full-time and rents a small apartment with her roommate. Unfortunately for both of them, Erica has never been very good at managing her money. She never knows how much money she has in her chequing or savings accounts, and her unpaid cell phone and credit card bills are always stuffed inside her purse or into the glove compartment of her car. Often, her debit/ATM card and credit cards are declined at stores. Erica jokes with her friends that she never knows when her phone bill is due until her cellphone service is cut off. This is funny enough until she gets stuck on the highway with a broken-down car and no cell phone service to enable her to call for help.

Erica needs to get organized! If you read the last paragraph with a sinking feeling in the pit of your stomach, don't worry. It's never too late to start!

File Folders Are Your Friends

If you don't track your money, you're going to lose it. So the first step in your organization process should be to set up a file-folder system, whether electronically or using good old-fashioned paper file folders. If you're like me, and some of your important documents are still sent to you by snail mail, you may need a tracking system that is a combination of both electronic and paper. If you go the paper route, head to your local office supply store and purchase multicoloured folders, labels, and an accordion case or one of those desktop hanging-folder contraptions.

Files are important because they allow you to separate and manage all the paperwork pertaining to the different areas that affect your financial, personal, and career life. Filing also gives you an opportunity to review your financial and personal information more carefully.

Here are some examples of file names that might be relevant for you:

- Bank statements (if you have more than one account, make a file for each and include the account number or type of account on the tab for easy reference)

- Utility bills, such as electricity, gas, and water (again, one folder for each utility)

- Cell phone bills

- Receipts

- Credit card bills and related materials

- Pay statements

- Tax/government-related materials

- Investment statements

- Resumés and letters of reference

- Health information

- Certificates of achievement

- School information

- School expenses

- Employment information

This should be enough to get you started. As you work your way through the stacks of important papers in your dresser drawers or on your desk, you'll probably find other materials that should be given a file. But don't get too carried away! You don't need a file for every piece of paper that makes its way into your home. A rule of thumb: file only the things that are important to you and that could significantly affect your life.

When you organize your files, put them into an order that makes sense to you — alphabetical, most frequently used, whatever. Just choose a system that will allow you to remember where things go.

The Not-So-Dreaded Spreadsheet

Although some people run screaming at the thought, a truly great way to get organized with your finances is to set up budgets using a computer-ized spreadsheet program (chapter 4 has more information on budget-ing). Most software packages come with a basic spreadsheet program, and that's all you really need. It allows you to insert formulas to add and subtract numbers automatically, or dates to assist you in planning for certain purchases.

You can also use your computer to create a list of "big-ticket items" that you can work toward purchasing as time progresses. For example, you could list items like a bicycle ($350) or car repairs ($900) or a down payment on a house ($10,000). Similar to what I suggested in chapter 1, put your list someplace where you'll see it on a daily basis (I have mine taped to my desk at home). It will help motivate you and keep you focused on your goals.

Let Technology Work for You

Getting organized with your banking and investments is easy when you have online access to your accounts. All you have to do is log on for a few minutes to check your investments, your bank balances, pay your bills, whatever! Make sure you register for your bank's online services (you may need to see a customer service representative to do this). If you've started to invest, you can use the Internet to track the performance of almost any stock, bond, mutual fund, or index or exchange-traded fund. Some good sites are:

- *www.bloomberg.com*

- *www.finance.yahoo.com*

- *www.globeinvestor.com*

- *www.morningstar.com*

Most North American financial services companies, such as banks, have a website containing all the relevant financial information for your banking and investments.

These websites, and others like them, include graphs showing the historical performance of your investments. They also include information to help you determine if a particular investment would be good for you. Some websites even allow you to download data for creating your own graphs in spreadsheet programs.

Twenty Minutes a Week

Getting a handle on your money doesn't take much more than a little planning and checking up once a week. If you're willing to take 20 minutes out of your busy week to devote to your financial future, I can guarantee you success. How many hours a day do you spend on social media, surfing YouTube, watching Netflix or television? If you are like most North Americans in our age group, you are glued to your electronics for 6 to 10 hours a day! That's between 42 and 70 hours per week![5] If you cut back 20 minutes per week of Instagram or Facebook and spend that time checking in on your money and learning more about how to make it, grow it, and spend it wisely, you can become a self-made millionaire.

With the 20 minutes you manage to free up, you could:

- Review your banking transactions. This will help you keep track of your expenses and income to ensure that you aren't overspending.

- Brush up your investment skills. Read a book about money management or surf financial websites or the business section of your local paper.

- Keep tabs on how your investments are doing.

- Set up your automatic banking transactions for the coming week.

THE BIG BAD BANK

Nineteen-year-old Kumar is in his second year of college. He hides half of his savings in the box his Apple LED Cinema monitor came in two years ago. The other half can be found in a small box in his closet. At any given time, he has a stash of more than $9,000 cash hidden in his room. Because he can easily access his money, he considers this technique more financially convenient than a bank.

Despite often getting a bad rap, banks are not evil. In fact, a good relationship with a bank you're comfortable with is a key component in your getting-organized campaign — as important as that filing system I recommended earlier.

As convenient as it may seem to have money sitting under your hard drive, it isn't very safe. There are way too many risks associated with keeping your money "under your mattress" rather than in a bank account. What if your house was robbed? What if your roof leaked? You could lose everything! Besides, if your money is sitting in your closet, it isn't earning interest, is it? And if you read chapter 1 carefully, you now know how important compounded interest and reinvested returns can be. The best place for your money is in an account where you can monitor its activity and earn interest.

Setting Up an Account

If you haven't already set up a bank account for yourself, now is the time. The first step is to pick a bank or institution that you would like to deal with.

There are large banks like RBC Royal Bank (Canada) or Bank of America (U.S.), or local banks like Vancity Bank in Vancouver or Columbia State Bank in Seattle. Most of the larger banks are owned by shareholders, whereas some of the smaller banks — typically credit unions — are privately owned or owned by the collective group of their customers. And Internet banks, like Tangerine (formerly known as ING Direct and now Capital One 360 in the U.S.), are becoming more popular because they have lower fees due to low overhead as they generally don't have a network of brick-and-mortar branches.

When selecting a bank, consider fees, location, convenience, policies, and customer service. Check out their websites and pay attention to word-of-mouth reputation. It can also be very helpful to get a referral from someone you trust, like your parents or a close friend.

Once you've selected the institution with which you'd like to deal, it's time to set up your accounts. If you are under 18, you may need to bring a parent or guardian along. You'll also need at least two pieces of up-to-date identification (a driver's licence, birth certificate, passport, or Social Security (USA) or Social Insurance (Canada) card, for example). Finally, be aware that some financial institutions require a minimum deposit of up to $100 on the day you open your account. Once you have all of that in order, an account representative or personal banker will help you determine what type of account will best suit your needs.

Chequing Accounts

A chequing account is designed for activity. Typically, people have their paycheques deposited into it and pay their bills and spend out of it.

As the name would suggest, you are also able to write cheques from it (but paper cheques have largely been replaced by email or Interac money transfer technology where you can electronically transfer funds from your bank account to another person's email through your online banking). A chequing account generally doesn't receive any deposit interest, which makes it less than ideal for long-term savings. Use a chequing account if you are likely to spend your money within two months of depositing it.

Because of the activity associated with chequing accounts, there is usually a service fee to be paid. When I was a student, I had to pay $3.50 each month to use my account. That banking package gave me 25 transactions per month and free online banking. Now I pay $14 per month for my chequing account. For that, I get 65 transactions per month, free online banking, free money orders, free email money transfers, and new paper cheques when I need them. This usually meets my needs. But many online banks are offering no-fee chequing accounts, and I'm a huge believer in free services.

Whether you go with an online or brick-and-mortar bank, it's worthwhile looking into these service packages when opening an account. Otherwise, you might find yourself paying some hefty fees (up to one dollar per transaction!). You can find information about banking packages online or by calling your bank's toll-free customer service number.

Savings Accounts

A savings account is designed as a place you can park your money for a longer period of time. You receive interest on the money that you have sitting in this account, but it isn't very much. Generally, it's worth thinking of your savings account as a place to put money that you will have for between two months and one year. For example, I save money for my yearly holidays in a savings account, but I don't put my retirement savings there. Savings accounts have fees associated with them only if you use them actively to withdraw money. This is to hinder you from spending your savings. The fees are typically higher than for a chequing account (sometimes up to three dollars per transaction), making it worth your while not to pull money out too frequently.

I highly recommend that you open both a chequing and a savings account. It's almost impossible to save for the long term in the same account that you use for daily banking activity. Separating your money will make your financial life much easier (you won't accidentally spend your savings!) and help you to develop healthy financial habits.

Debit/ATM Cards and Online/Telephone Access

When you are in the process of opening your chequing and savings accounts, think about whether you want or need a debit/ATM card. This card allows you to pay for your purchases directly from your bank account at the stores where you shop and gives you ATM access to your various accounts. It also makes online and telephone banking possible. Debit/ATM cards can be wonderfully convenient. Unfortunately, they can also tempt you to spend too much money.

If you're given a choice, I recommend getting a card that allows access to your chequing account but not your savings account. That way, you'll have the convenience of accessing your money when you need it, but you won't end up touching your savings. As your comfort level with money increases, you might want to consider allowing yourself ATM access to your savings, but only for the purpose of depositing funds into your account and for emergency withdrawals.

I'm a huge proponent of working off the cash system, where you pay cash for your purchases in an attempt to curb overspending, and only use your debit/ATM card when you need to withdraw the cash you require for the week. However, if you feel you'd like to use your debit/ATM card for purchases, keep a tally of your spending by collecting your receipts and checking your accounts online so that you can manage your spending and avoid running out of money. Then, when your bank statements show up, cross-reference your receipts with your statements. This will ensure there is no funny business going on with the account.

Lastly, get access to online and telephone banking services so you can manage your day-to-day banking and investing.

A Banking Checklist

Here's a quick to-do list to keep in mind when opening your accounts:

- Choose a bank or institution that suits your needs.

- Make an appointment with a financial adviser, the person who will open your accounts, ahead of time.

- Bring along Mom, Dad, or a legal guardian (if you're under 18).

- Bring at least two pieces of current identification.

- Ask to open both a chequing and a savings account.

- Research your bank's service packages and find the one that works for you.

- Be prepared to make a minimum deposit.

- Get a debit/ATM card and set it up with access to your chequing account ONLY.

- Set up online and telephone banking.

BUYER BEWARE!

When you visit the bank to open your new accounts, don't be surprised if the financial adviser tries to "sell" you a credit card. Avoid the temptation to sign up — at least for now. You'll find a lot more information on credit cards in chapter 5.

Fees, Fees, and More Fees

Many people go ballistic over the service fees they pay their banks. Maybe that's because we all know how much money banks are raking in. Let's face it — at least some of that profit is coming out of your account, if not via fees than through the interest they earn by using your money for their own investments.

It's worth keeping in mind, though, that the fees you pay don't "buy" a physical product. They buy a service. After all, financial institutions have to staff their various departments in order to serve you and their other clients. They transfer a portion of that cost down to you. Banks that provide a high level of customer service tend to charge higher fees; those that operate on more of a "self-serve" basis charge less.

To get a clear picture of how this works, let's compare an online bank like Capital One 360 (Tangerine) to Bank of America. When you have an account with Capital One 360 (Tangerine), there are far fewer people to serve you because they have fewer branch locations. There is limited "service" available, except by phone and online, therefore there are few service fees. In fact, Capital One 360 (Tangerine) typically doesn't charge fees on savings accounts. On the other hand, Bank of America offers teller services as well as many other account services. For example, you could meet with someone in person or on the phone to talk about your banking card limits, loans, mortgages, investments, et cetera. You can talk to a representative if and when you want. Not surprisingly, this service costs money.

A similar situation exists with brokerage or trading accounts for your investments. Let's say you are a very confident investor and you've been investing in the stock market for many years. You make your own investment decisions without the influence of your broker or financial planner. You don't need, or want, to pay for their advice. You'd be best served by an online trading account that allows you to trade what, when, and where you want, all for as low as $9.99 per transaction. However, an investor who doesn't want the hassle, or has less knowledge or confidence, might prefer to use a full-service broker, regardless of the fee (which can be a percentage of funds invested or upward of $300 per transaction).

In the end, how you feel about service fees will likely depend on your priorities. Do you value high customer service levels or not? If you choose to go with a bank that charges service fees, make sure that you are getting good service for your money. If at any time you feel that you are being let down by the customer service representatives, feel free to speak up. The consumer — regardless of his or her age — is very powerful! Good institutions will recognize and respect that. People in the banking services industry should want to help guide young customers down the path of financial security. If they aren't willing to support you in your banking and investing endeavors, they don't deserve your business.

Advisers and Other Bankers

When you arrive at whichever financial institution you've chosen, a financial adviser will assist you in setting up your accounts. Financial advisers can handle most non-transaction account services. For example, they can assist in choosing and setting up the best accounts for your needs, selecting the proper service-fee package, and setting up your debit/ATM card. Often, financial advisers will also be able to set up basic investments. They can ask you questions about your long- and short-term goals to help determine which basic investments will suit your needs.

By the time you're finished this book, you'll likely be able to start putting together your own financial plan without the help of an adviser. However, when you've got a good handle on the basics, it is great to get some advice from a financial adviser. Financial advisers often share good ideas for your money, and the more information you have, the better. They also tend to approach your personal money management in a very organized manner. Knowledge is a very powerful tool. I'd highly recommend sitting down with one to work out a plan that works for you and balances between your financial, personal, and career goals.

Wondering where to find a great adviser? Start by asking friends and family members for personal referrals. Then go and interview at least three advisers to see if you "click" with any. If it feels right, work with them. But check in regularly to ensure you're getting the results and level of service you expect.

CHAPTER 4
Get Started: The Bu-Bu-Bu-Budget

Now that you're organized (or at least on your way to being organized), it's time to start properly managing your money. And the first step in this process is a budget. Unfortunately, budgets have a bad reputation — they take a lot of time, they're restrictive, et cetera.

Yup, I'd be in denial if I didn't admit a lot of people — especially people our age — don't like to think about budgets. Yes, I understand that the whole idea is kind of boring, and it does seem to suggest that huge compromises will need to be made regarding your spending. Well, the second part may be partially true (small compromises will likely need to be made), but budgeting isn't boring; it's essential. And you can build fun right into your budget. A good budget is a vital first step on the road to financial success. Without one, it's next to impossible to know where your money is coming from or where it's going. Self-made millionaires, many of whom I have had the opportunity to consult with, cite budgeting as a critical component of their financial success. Preparing a budget isn't difficult, and you can think of the exercise as very little pain now for a whole lot of gain later.

Frugality is different from being a cheapskate. Frugal people use budgets as a tool to stretch their dollars as far as they can go, without compromising on quality. They're the people that split the tab; not run out on it. Cheapskates, on the other hand, will do anything to save a buck because they haven't budgeted properly. Often, they spend more money in the long-run replacing shoddy products.

DON'T BE LATE

The only time developing a budget can get tricky is if you do it too late. Let's say you're on a road trip with your friends. You drive for five hours and arrive at the hotel. You pay for the room, go out for a fancy dinner, do some shopping, and put a little more gas in the car. As you merrily spend away, no one stops to think about how much money is left in your communal "bank." What happens the next day when the car breaks down and you're out of money? You can avoid this situation by creating a simple budget, and sticking to it, before you start any adventure.

THE 411 ON BUDGETING

A budget is a financial statement or document outlining your income and expenditures over a specific period of time. Think of it as a plan for your money — and remember that it doesn't have to be complicated. All you really need to prepare a budget is the spreadsheet software that came with your computer. You could also draft one up on graph paper, but then you'll have to do all the adding and subtracting yourself. To prove just how easy it really is, I'm going to walk through how you can create your own personal budget.

Income and Expenses
First things first. Any budget — be it corporate, household, or personal

— begins with an examination of income. Where's the money coming from? For corporations, answering this question can be an extremely complex exercise; for you, it shouldn't be that hard.

Below are a few examples of the "income" portion of a budget. First is the monthly budget of Noor, a 17-year-old high school student; second is the budget of Peter, a 25-year-old financial analyst at a construction company. Both budgets are based on a one-month period of time.

NOOR (STUDENT)

Sources of Income	Income ($)
Part-time job	500
Small side jobs	50
TOTAL	**550**

PETER (FINANCIAL ANALYST)

Sources of Income	Income ($)
Full-time job	2,800
Freelance work (after hours)	50
TOTAL	**2,850**

So far, so good. Now, think about your situation. Do you have a full- or part-time job? Do you earn an allowance for doing chores around the house? Do you receive money from the government? You need to take into account any money you've got coming in. In the case of your personal budget, the income is based on after-tax dollars. Now, fill in and total up the "income" portion of your own budget in the worksheet below or in your spreadsheet program. You may wish to set up a quarterly, monthly, or biweekly budget. Most people select a monthly time frame to correspond with their paycheques and bills.

MY INCOME

Sources of Income	Income ($)

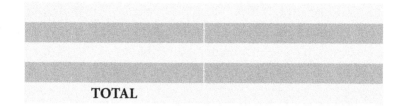

TOTAL	

Once you have your total income figured out, it's time to look at your expenses. What do you spend money on every month? You need to think about everything — from big-picture stuff like car loans and rent, to little things like coffee and lunches in the school cafeteria. Keeping track of your expenses is the cornerstone of your financial well-being. One of the top reasons that people (and businesses) go bankrupt is improper cash flow management. Simply put, more money ends up going out than coming in. Not a good scene!

Let's get back to Noor and Peter and have a look at their monthly expenditures.

NOOR (STUDENT)

Expenses	Expenditures ($)
Clothing	50
Food	50
Savings	50
Entertainment	100
School	150
TOTAL	**400**

PETER (FINANCIAL ANALYST)

Expenses	Expenditures ($)
Mortgage	850
Student loan	300
Credit card payment	200
Groceries	200

Investment account	100
Heat/cooling	100
Taxes	100
Electricity	100
Home association fees (condo)	100
Insurance (home, auto, medical)	150
Transit/metro pass	100
Vehicle fuel	100
Subtotal of mandatory expenses	**2,400**
Furniture payment	100
Cell phone bill	50
Cable, phone, Internet	100
Gym membership	50
Fun money	200
Subtotal of secondary expenses	**500**
TOTAL	**2,900**

A couple of notes on the categories in Peter's budget. Mandatory expenses are things that you literally cannot live without. You'll notice that investments are in this category. Yes, your financial security is *that* important. Secondary expenses, on the other hand, are things that you could live without if push came to shove. They tend to be things we value that make our lives a bit easier and more fun like travel or gifts for others. You'll note that Peter has built fun expenses into this category. Now it's your turn. Use the worksheet below or your spreadsheet to fill in your own monthly expenses.

BUDGET BUSTERS

The largest budget busters for most under-thirties are meals out, electronics and clothes. What's your spending vice? Don't let it ruin your financial future. Set a clear limit on what you plan to spend on your biggest budget buster each month. Try to find coupons to use towards it, buy second-hand or DIY.

MY EXPENDITURES

Expenses	Expenditures ($)
Mandatory expenses	
Sub-total of mandatory expenses	
Secondary expenses	
Sub-total of secondary expenses	
TOTAL	

We're down to the final piece of the puzzle now — blending the income portion of your budget with the expenses portion. Subtract the total expenses from the total income to get to your bottom line — and yes, it actually is the bottom line of the budget, so that's where the term "bottom line" comes from.

Total income - Total expenses = Bottom line

If you are spending less than you're making, you have a surplus. If you are spending more than you're making, which is not a good idea, you have a loss. Here are Noor's and Peter's completed budgets:

NOOR (STUDENT)

Sources of Income	Income ($)
Part-time job	500
Small side jobs	50
Total income	**550**
Expenses	Expenditures ($)
Clothing	50
Food	50
Savings	50
Entertainment	100
School	150
Total expenses	**400**
Bottom line	**$150**

PETER (FINANCIAL ANALYST)

Sources of Income	Income ($)
Full-time job	2,800
Freelance work (after hours)	50
Total income	**2,850**
Expenses	Expenditures ($)
Mortgage	850
Student loan	300

Credit card payment	200
Groceries	200
Investment account	100
Heat/cooling	100
Taxes	100
Electricity	100
Home association fees (condo)	100
Insurance (home, auto, medical)	150
Transit/metro pass	100
Vehicle fuel	100
Subtotal of mandatory expenses	**2,400**
Furniture payment	100
Cell phone bill	50
Cable, phone, Internet	100
Gym membership	50
Fun money	200
Subtotal of secondary expenses	**500**
Total expenses	**2,900**
Bottom line	**-50**

Noor is doing very well. Her bottom line is $150 every month. With this "surplus" money, she could grow her savings, take a trip, save up for a new iPad Mini, pay for school supplies, and so much more — the bottom line, no pun intended, is that she has options. Peter, on the other hand, isn't faring so well. He's looking at a net monthly loss — a.k.a. a *deficit* — of $50. The big problem with running a loss each month, even if it's small, like in Peter's situation, is that over the course of many months, it adds up. To cover his losses each month, Peter has to borrow money from either his credit card or bank overdraft. Clearly, something's not working for Peter. After paying his mandatory expenses each month, there's hardly any money left over. When he layers in his "nice-to-haves," he's running in the red. To correct this situation, lifestyle changes are likely needed — a roommate, perhaps, or a move to cheaper accommodations, the sale of his ratty old vehicle to reduce fuel and insurance costs, et cetera. Whatever path Peter chooses, his hands are tied; he either stops spending so much or he goes into debt further.

Now it's time to calculate your bottom line. Fill in the worksheet below and grab a calculator. It's a very simple exercise. Subtract your total expenses from your income to get to your bottom line.

MY BOTTOM LINE

Sources of Income	Income ($)
Total income	

Expenses	Expenditures ($)
Mandatory expenses	
Sub-total of mandatory expenses	

Secondary expenses

Sub-total of secondary expenses	
Total expenses	
Bottom line	

How did you do? Are you in a positive or negative position? Don't feel bad if your bottom line isn't looking great. You're certainly not alone, and part of the reason you bought this book was to help you get control of your financial life, right?

The bottom line of your budget should act as a guide for the next steps in your financial makeover. If the number is negative, you're over-spending. In financial circles, this is referred to as a **deficit**, and to say that it's generally frowned upon would be an understatement. If, on the other hand, your bottom line is positive, you're in a **surplus** situation — all in all a much happier place to be!

Surpluses are usually produced when a budget allots more money for a specific product or service than is actually needed. Imagine shopping for a cool new red sweater. You've done your research and you know that the sweater costs $40. You walk into your favourite store and discover that the sweater is 25 percent off. Instead of spending $40, you pay $30. You walk out of the store with the sweater and a $10 surplus in your pocket. Awesome!

The opposite situation occurs when you walk into the same store to find out that the sweater you saw last week for $40 now costs $50. You decide to buy it anyway, and now, you've created a $10 deficit.

The income tax process provides another useful example of these concepts. If your employer has taken too much tax off your paycheques throughout the year, you'll probably end up getting a nice tax return in the mail — a surplus. If he or she hasn't taken off enough, you'll end up owing money to the Canada Revenue Agency (Canada) or the Internal Revenue Service (U.S.) — a deficit.

So how do you cope with these situations? Read on.

ASSETS AND LIABILITIES

Open up another tab on your spreadsheet to calculate your **personal net worth** by listing your assets and liabilities. In financial terms, an **asset** refers to something that you own that grows in value — like a home, business, or investment. A **liability** generally refers to something that you owe money on, like a student loan, a car loan, a mortgage, or any other type of debt. When you subtract your liabilities from your assets, you are left with your **personal net worth** — and there's nothing more exciting than watching it grow over time!

UNDERSPENDING: A SURPLUS IS A WONDERFUL THING

Let's start with the best-case scenario. Your budget shows that you've got money left over at the end of each month. Congratulations! What are you going to do? Rush out and treat your ten closest friends to a night on the town? You might be able to afford it, but it wouldn't be the best plan in the long run.

Before visions of extra lattes and thousands of downloads start dancing through your head, think back to chapter 1 and your list of goals. What did you write down on page 22? You are now in the enviable position of having some extra cash to help make those dreams a reality.

When we get to chapter 6, we're going to talk specifically about how to save for items you want to buy in the short term. For now, simply remember that you should always put aside money when you can afford to do so. Here are a few tips to help get you started.

Tips for Dealing with a Surplus

If you are in the fortunate position of having a surplus, here are a few suggestions for what you might do with the extra cash:

- Start an automated savings plan so that you are saving and investing regularly.

- Pay down high-interest debts (see chapter 5).

- Start a college fund.

- Contribute to a down payment for your first home.

- Contribute to a retirement savings account, like an RRSP (Canada) or a 401(k) (U.S.) (see chapter 8).

- Reward yourself with part of the surplus ... NOT all of it.

IT'S OKAY TO REWARD YOURSELF

We've talked a lot about reining in your spending so that you don't cause yourself financial grief. But it's also important to take pride in your income earning ability and reward yourself. Sometimes those rewards come through spending your money on things that are important to you. For example, every year I try to reward myself with a vacation. I find great pleasure in taking a few weeks off and exploring, relaxing, and having fun.

OVERSPENDING: THE DANGERS OF DEFICITS

So, you're over your monthly budget. You are spending more than you're earning, which might explain why you're always having to borrow bus fare from your parents! What should you do? What *can* you do? You have three options: reduce your spending, increase your income, or borrow money. Obviously, this last option isn't a good one. So let's look at some tips that address the other two.

Tips for Dealing with a Deficit

- **Question everything.** Look carefully at your budget. What are your biggest expenses? Are you spending more money on clothes each month than you need to? Is your car insurance through the roof? Ask yourself if there are lifestyle changes you can make to reduce your monthly output of cash. Eliminating two pizza dinners each month, for example, could free up $35!

- **Look for opportunities to make more.** Do you have the ability to increase your income? Could you open a small business or join a multi-level marketing organization? Can you take on a few more hours at work or make a deal with your parents to do an additional household chore in exchange for an increase in your allowance? Could you return bottles or house-sit? Could you rent out a spare room? Are you driving friends to school every day? Might they be able to contribute a small amount to your gas costs? Do you have a hidden talent that you could make money with on the side? These things may seem insignificant, but every little bit helps.

- **Reorganize your priorities.** Put your savings and investing goals at the very top of your list of expenses. These should be non-negotiable — more important to you than a few extra cable channels or an extra night out. Always pay yourself first because no one else will — even if it's only $25 a month.

- **Examine your cash flow.** As much as we'd like them to be fixed in stone, our expenses change from month to month. This affects your **cash flow** — how much money comes into and goes out of your bank account each month. You need to be aware of these fluctuations in order to have a firm grasp on your spending habits. For example, people tend to spend more in December because of the holidays. If you don't budget for this, you might end up with a big credit card bill near the end of January. The opposite can also occur. Are you taking a two-week holiday from work in the summer? Include your transportation costs to go on your trip, like a plane ticket or fuel for your vehicle, in your budget for that month. The more aware you are of these fluctuations, the better you'll be able to handle them.

- **Plan for emergencies.** While you're revamping your budget, it's not a bad idea to include an expense dedicated to building an emergency fund. If your car broke down tomorrow, would you have enough money to fix it? If you lost your job next week, how would you cover your expenses until you could find a new one?

  Late in 2013 I had to have reconstructive jaw surgery after a hiking accident where I essentially tripped, fell into a hole, smacked my head, and broke my jaw. I didn't know it right away, but my medical insurance covered only a small fraction of the costs for my full treatment. I had to fork out the rest — to the tune of nearly $45,000. I wasn't expecting that expense and I had to clear out my emergency fund to pay for my treatment. I was thankful I had the money. Now I'm rebuilding my "rainy day"/emergency fund.

  No one likes to spend more than they have, but things happen. Often, people don't plan for the unexpected. When an emergency occurs, they end up having to work overtime, pay high interest rates on a credit card, or do without something they really need. Some experts recommend that you sock away the equivalent of six months' salary in your own emergency fund. That's a little excessive for the average person, so choose a number that you find comfortable. Then, work it into your short-term savings plan (see chapter 6).

- **Avoid debt.** Only as an absolute last resort should you borrow money to cover your expenses. We'll talk lots more about debt in chapter 5, but for now, just know that borrowing to pay for something you can't really afford is the first step down a very slippery slope. Before long, you'll be borrowing to pay off what you've already borrowed, and so on and so forth. It's much better to look at what you're buying and ask yourself if you really need it. You'll be surprised at how often the answer is "no."

AVOIDING HOME POVERTY

When I graduated from university, I bought a townhome. I was so excited about having a new job, a new home, living on my own — the whole package! Before too long, however, I ran right into an extremely common trap: home poverty. Basically, all I could afford was my house! I didn't have much money left over for anything else. Home poverty is a common phenomenon among under-30s as the cost of living and house prices have increased rapidly. But it's a highly restrictive scenario and one that can be avoided through savvy budgeting, by purchasing a smaller and more affordable house, by borrowing less money, and by planning ahead for major household maintenance expenses, like the eventual replacement of a water tank.

BUDGETS CAN PREVENT BANKRUPTCY

On paper, someone like me makes a healthy income, but if I don't carefully monitor my cash flow, especially what I spend on my housing, I could end up like many North Americans — bankrupt! Let's look at how this can happen, using Peter from our previous budgeting example. Peter recently bought a small condominium and still has some student loans to pay off. Although he has a great job, he's still running out of money every month and accumulating a deficit of approximately $50 per month — this adds up! Typically in December, around the holidays, and in July, when he takes summer vacation, Peter's budget takes a turn for the worse — furthering his deficit. That's because in both instances, he spends beyond his normal budget by purchasing gifts and plane tickets. Here is a running tally of his overspending for the year.

PETER'S OVERSPENDING

Month	Monthly Deficit ($)	Accumulated Deficit ($)
January	50	50
February	50	100
March	50	150
April	50	200
May	50	250
June	50	300
July	500	800
August	50	850
September	50	900
October	50	950
November	50	1,000
December	500	1,500
TOTAL		**1,500**

You can see that by the end of the year, Peter's accumulated deficit has grown to $1,500, and that's because every month he can't afford to pay off his existing deficit before more plows over him. And without a plan to stop overspending, it will continue to grow — it has a snowball effect. Imagine what this growing deficit will add up to in a few years' time!

What's worse is that the deficit turns into debt because Peter will have to borrow money to cover his expenses. In his case, he'll use the overdraft protection provided by his bank account, at a whopping 22 percent interest rate, to finance his overspending — that's a higher rate than even the most commonly used credit cards. Debt builds on top of debt, thus creating more debt.

Scary, isn't it? Peter presents a perfect example of what can happen if you don't set realistic budgets, stick to your cash flow goals, and quickly rectify overspending. The accumulation of monthly deficits, which turn into debt, ultimately cause bankruptcy.

If you're running in the red month after month, here are some ideas to help you stop overspending and tackle your accumulated deficit.

- **Consider finding a roommate** with whom you can split the rent/mortgage, utilities, and grocery bills.

- **Follow recommended heating and electricity practices** to help reduce your monthly bills. For example, turn off your lights and computer before you head off for work. Also, ensure that you have the proper weather stripping on all of your doors and windows. If you're renting, ask your landlord to do this for you.

- **Cut the cable.** Who needs it anyway when you have the Internet — just watch out for high fees for streaming video! Better yet, grab a book or rent movies from the library.

- **Perform your own maintenance.** You'd be surprised at the number of people who pay others to do things they could actually do themselves. Hey, if you feel entrepreneurial, you could make money doing other people's housecleaning, lawn maintenance, leaf raking, or snow shovelling.

- **Get rid of unnecessary items.** Craigslist, eBay, and Kijiji are wonderful places to get rid of things you don't need. It is also a way for you to gain additional income from the sale of unnecessary things.

- **Downsize.** If your house is too big or your car is too fancy, downsize them, and your expectations.

- **Buy used.** If you need to replace something in your home, purchase it used. Often you can save hundreds, if not thousands, of dollars this way.

Debt has the ability to stop all your financial, personal, and career progress, so the following chapter will show you how to avoid a credit crunch.

CHAPTER 5
Get Out from Under: Avoiding the Credit Crunch

FROM BROKE TO BALI

A few years ago, I became friends with a super-cool gal, 27-year-old Chelsea. We clicked immediately when we learned of our mutual interest in money management. Chelsea used to be broke — as in, not-two-nickels-to-rub-together kind of broke — and heavily in debt. She'd taken out student loans totalling over $20,000 in her early 20s and had racked up $15,000 on her credit card so that she could backpack her way through Europe after university.

When Chelsea returned home from her awesome European adventures, she learned three tough financial lessons. The first was that it was harder than she thought to get a good job, given she had little to no experience. The second was that she had no practical work experience to accompany her educational training in psychology and arts. This make her uncompetitive in a market where other students had done work terms with the government, businesses, and non-profits. The third lesson was that her debt was going to hold her back from getting the things she wanted in life.

In and around the same time she started having these revelations, Chelsea was living in Vancouver and met her dream guy: Conner, a hip skateboarding Canadian who had a successful business making surf clothes in Bali. His lifestyle was enviable — a wicked profession, low cost of living, ocean, palm trees, fresh seafood literally outside his front door, and a scooter to get him from point A to point B. In and around their fourth date, Conner suggested that Chelsea clean up her finances.

After a little probing on Chelsea's part, she quickly connected the dots. Her awesome dude wanted her to have the financial flexibility to come visit and potentially live with him in Bali.

Shortly thereafter she traded in her job as an assistant to an interior home designer for one in the corporate social responsibility department of a large corporation, increasing her salary by one-third. Sure, she had to work longer hours, but the pay made it worth her while. Next, Chelsea advertised on Kijiji that she was a professional house-sitter. Clients snapped her up instantaneously. She essentially started to live for free, caring for other people's homes and pets. She also collected a paycheque for this. Chelsea then joined a multi-level marketing organization, selling skin care products to earn more income.

Every month that went by, Chelsea lived frugally, couponing for everything and resisting the temptation to overspend whenever she got the urge to. Chelsea put every penny she could toward her debts.

Over the course of three years, Chelsea became debt-free. Sadly, I had to say goodbye to her when she officially moved to Bali in 2014, but it was with great joy that we toasted her incredible accomplishment!

What's Your Bali?

If there's one thing that can put the brakes on a good financial plan and your hopes and dreams for the future, it's a whopping pile of debt. Let's take a few minutes to examine the debt factor: why we're in it, how to pay it down if we are, and, perhaps most importantly, how to avoid it altogether!

THE MONEY PIT

Money seriously doesn't grow on trees. As obvious as this may seem, and despite the rising costs of post-secondary education and high levels of unemployment and underemployment (working at jobs we're overqualified and underpaid for), our generation spends as if it does.[6] After so many of us watched our parents lose their jobs, retirement savings, and sometimes their houses during the financial crises of 2008 and 2009, we've adopted a YOLO — you only live once — culture. We want to enjoy life's finer things, like travel, food, and technology, earlier — just in case we can't afford these luxuries later. So, over the course of the past decade, the spending power of under-30s has increased substantially, to over $200 billion a year in North America. Research shops like Kelton Research have even suggested that Generation Y — yup, that's us — will outspend the baby boomers.[7]

The biggest challenge with us chasing our dreams so early in life is that we don't actually have the money to afford our adventures — just like Chelsea. This has made us the most indebted generation ever!

Thus, many of us have managed our financial pressures, namely boat-loads of student and consumer debt, by living at home longer, avoiding large purchases such as a home, delaying marriage, and trying to make more money through entrepreneurship.

The teen market is also huge into spending, with the average 12- to 13-year-old spending $1,500 each year, while the average 16- to 17-year-old spends $4,500. That's a lot of money! In fact, teens today have more spending money than their parents, who have to pay for things like housing, heat, and electricity.

In either situation, be it living at home in your 20s or being a teen-ager, having fewer household financial obligations typically translates into a tendency to spend our money on things that we want, rather than on things that we need.

How We Get Sucked In

Keaton, 21, and Claire, 22, have been dating for six months. On the week-ends — when they aren't working shifts or cramming in studies — you can usually find them at the mall, shopping online, or socializing with friends at their local pub. Neither pays rent to their parents, so shopping for the things they love — food, music, clothes, or electronics — is gen-erally within their budget. It isn't uncommon for each of them to spend $200 in a weekend.

Like Keaton and Claire, many of us under-30s spend thousands of dollars consuming things we don't need. Some of the largest culprits are coffee, nightclubs, alcohol, taxis, food, clothes, electronics, and trips.

Why are we spending so much? There are some very powerful marketing and advertising forces out there! The amount of money spent on retail advertising has increased every year for decades. Globally, in 2014 ad spending reached approximately $550 billion, with digital advertising comprising approximately one-quarter of that sum. North America's share of the digital advertising market was approximately 40 percent.[8] No wonder we're compelled to shop! Advertising messages are extremely convincing, and they all say the same thing: "You NEED to have this service or product, and you need to have it NOW."

Our generation can end up trapped in debt because of so-called retail therapy. Swayed by all of this advertising, we shop to make ourselves happy. We watch beer commercials and think that if we drink that brand, we'll live that kind of life. We buy skin cream because we want to look like the model in the ad. We're chasing the dreams that the advertising companies put out there for us, and we like doing it! We tend to be happy with our purchases — at least until that credit card bill arrives.

Further, our generation has a strange fascination with having the same things that "rich" people have — this is the phenomenon of "keeping up with the Joneses." The Joneses are popular. They rove around in fancy cars, wear stylish clothes, live in expensive homes, frequent local hot spots, and have equally cool boyfriends, girlfriends, or spouses hanging off their arms.

But they are broke, so why try keeping up? That's right — behind all the glitz and glam, many "rich" under-30s are stressed out and can barely pay for their groceries. That's because in their attempt to look the part, these wannabe millionaires are up to their eyeballs in debt. The way they keep up the façade is through low minimum monthly payments on their credit cards and loans. What many don't realize is that high interest charges can really add up. These people don't actually have wealth.

True self-made millionaires live within their means, and that isn't always flashy or snazzy — in the majority of cases, it's a choice to live frugally and humbly.

Though marketing and advertising forces are strong, as is the peer pressure to fit in with friends, you can turn the tables and use these forces to your advantage — as a source of knowledge rather than persuasion.

When you're in the market for a car, for example, do some research into what's out there. Use advertisements and word-of-mouth recommendations to find out more about a given vehicle (price, safety, quality, et cetera). You can then compare models and brands. With any medium or large product or service that you want to purchase, it is a good idea to do some research and get your facts in order so that you can make the best decision for you.

Shopping around can actually be quite fun. When I was in university, my friend Laura was in the market for a car. She had been driving around in a "beater" for years and finally had saved enough to purchase a quality used car. Laura took a few months to make a decision about which vehicle to buy. She searched the Internet for quality and safety ratings. She spoke with friends who had vehicles she might be interested in. She test drove her "picks" a number of times. Slowly, she narrowed down her search to her two favourite cars. She then began speaking with dealerships and private sellers about price. She chose an Acura that was a great deal. Because she didn't buy new, she saved money. Because she took the time to negotiate, she saved money. Lastly, because she did her research, she saved money by not getting ripped off. Laura was the very happy owner of a car she loved.

Debt, Debt, and More Debt: The Dangers of Interest and Credit Cards

So we've established that spending money is fun — we like to buy things that we want and need. And it's clear that most of us are pretty good at it, too! All we need to do is think of something we want, find it, purchase it, and voilà, the money is spent.

That's the happy side of the coin. The scary side is that we often don't have the money needed to make the purchase. But we make the purchase anyway. How? We go into debt.

Because credit is so readily available, we've become very comfortable with the idea of owing money. Most of us have credit cards, and we don't hesitate to use them. We live in a "buy now, pay later" society, and we fully expect to get the things we crave without having to wait or save up. We throw the purchase on the credit card and have to work extra hours so that we can pay for our fancy new items. What's worse, these fancy new items end up costing us more than we should really be paying. If we can't pay the bill in full at the end of the month, the credit card company charges us interest, usually between 17 and 20 percent. Remarkably, many store credit cards charge even higher interest rates — some in the range of 28 or 29 percent. The nastiest part about the whole thing is that typically, credit card companies compound their interest charges daily — not monthly. Now that happy feeling we got from instant gratification has forced us into a situation where we are continually paying for the past rather than investing in the future! Doesn't feel so good anymore, does it?

Take a minute to really look at this phenomenon. Let's say that you purchase a few new outfits from your favourite online retailer at a cost of $600. Let's also say that you pay for them with your credit card, which charges you 19.5 percent interest. The minimum payment on the bill you receive is likely about 3 percent of your total balance, meaning 3 percent of $600, or $18 (depending on your interest rate, the card, and the credit agreement — most credit cards will have a minimum payment set between 2 and 6 percent of the balance owed or $10 — whichever is the higher value). Because of the way interest is calculated on credit cards (compounded daily), if you make only the minimum payment, you'll barely be covering the interest! Almost none of your payment will go toward the principle amount owing. If you were to stick to this approach — paying only the original minimum payment of $18 per month — it would take you approximately 49 months to pay off that initial $600. Even worse, the "true" cost of your borrowing (principle plus interest paid) would be just over $870! That's $270 in interest! What a waste of your hard-earned money.

Biweekly and Accelerated Biweekly Payments

A **biweekly payment** is very beneficial with large debts, like mortgages and car payments, because it allows you to accelerate the payment process. For argument's sake, let's say you currently pay $1,000 per month as a mortgage payment. If you pay half the regular monthly payment, $500 every two weeks (biweekly) instead of paying $1000 once a month, you end up paying $13,000 every year versus $12,000. That is because there are 26 biweekly payments (52 weeks divided by 2-week intervals) of $500 each. The reason why biweekly payments are so popular is that you end up reducing the amount of time it takes to pay down that debt because you're chipping away at more principle, the original big amount, and therefore you save money on interest costs. In addition to this, many North Americans are paid biweekly, so they can align their payments with their paycheques.

Now, paying an extra $1,000 every year means you have to find that money somewhere. But when you divide that amount over the course of 12 months, it isn't nearly as big a pill to swallow. You might, however, have to cut back on a few lattes or switch to a less expensive gym.

There is nothing magical about biweekly payments. It's just another opportunity to put more money on your debt by squeezing in a higher payment than normal.

Reducing your debt with an **accelerated biweekly payment** allows you to put more of your coin on the principle amount owing, rather than on the accrued interest. Accelerated biweekly payment is simply a slightly higher payment. For example, rather than paying $500 every two weeks, you would pay $505. By doing so, you end up reducing your debt faster than you would if you made regular biweekly or even monthly payments. In most instances, these types of payments can be set up by your lender. But you can achieve the same result by logging into your online banking and adding a little extra to your regular payment.

Let's say that you're carrying a $40,000 balance on your credit card (extreme, I know, but it will help make a point). On that amount of debt, your minimum monthly payment would be at least $800 or 2 percent of your balance owing. In the initial stages of your payments, with an interest rate of 19.5 percent, approximately $650 of that payment would be applied to interest penalties and only $150 to the principle debt. As time passes, and if you carry on paying $800 each month, more of your payment goes toward the principle and less toward interest expenses. At this rate, you'd be looking at just under nine years' worth of payments before you were debt-free, with total interest paid of $43,000! That's more than the original balance owing! The primary reason it is so expensive to carry a balance is because credit card companies take the interest rate you pay, divide it by 365 days and compound it *each day*!

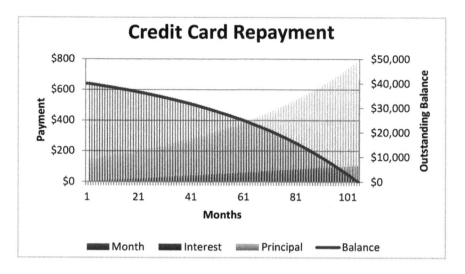

If, however, you can pay off your balance within 30 days, you don't pay any interest at all. Before you whip out that card, think about whether you can afford to pay it off. If it's going to take you months to clear your balance, you might want to hold off on your purchase. Check out the credit card calculators on *www.bankrate.com* or *www.getsmarteraboutmoney.com*. These calculators allow you to determine the cost of carrying a credit card balance as well as how long it will take for you to pay it off.

OUT WITH THE BAD, IN WITH THE GOOD

Good debt is used for things that help you grow your assets — these are things that grow in value. So, for example, your student loan, which was used to invest in your education, which will help you make more money long term, is considered a good debt. A wisely used mortgage or investment loan would also be considered good debt. Bad debt, on the other hand, is used for things that don't grow in value, like a credit card purchase of new jeans or Coachella tickets. Bad debt is very expensive and restrictive; thus, you'll want to avoid bad debt and learn to manage good debt.

WHEN IS A CREDIT CARD A GOOD THING?

Credit cards aren't *all* bad. They can be very useful in building your credit rating. When you use credit, the credit bureaus evaluate how well you manage your credit. If you're responsible, meaning that you pay your bills on time and in full, your credit rating will be high. If you miss payments or are late in paying, you'll have a lower score. The higher your credit score, the more success you'll have in getting better interest rates on loans, mortgages, other credit cards, and the like. A lower score affects your ability to borrow money at good rates, get rental applications approved, and even sign up for things like cell phone plans. In Canada and the United States you are entitled to one free credit report each year from one of the three main credit bureaus: Equifax, TransUnion, or Experian. Due to an increase in identity theft, checking up on your credit score is wise so that you can quickly catch any fraud. Plus, knowing the status of your score will indicate whether you need to spend time improving it.

Your credit score impacts your life. To borrow money, you need proof you're responsible enough to pay it off. A credit card offers a good opportunity for you to show potential creditors that you can indeed manage debt responsibly.

A credit card also enables you to book vacations, shop online, pay tuition, et cetera. And it can be very useful if you run into trouble. For example, my car broke down one summer about 500 kilometres from home. I used my credit card to pay a mechanic to fix my car. I made it home safely and paid off my bill with my next paycheque.

DIGGING YOUR WAY OUT

Mike is a 30-year-old electrician's apprentice. Between ages 25 and 30, he managed to rack up about $30,000 in debt. Because he missed some payments, he got himself into a lot of financial trouble, making it very difficult for him to borrow at good interest rates. He is still paying off his debt.

Does Mike's situation sound familiar to you? Have you gotten yourself in over your head? Are you looking at a pile of credit card bills with no idea of how to pay them off? First, I'd suggest that you go back and reread the sections on living a frugal life. Trust me, it will help. The basic idea, though, is this: You need to reduce your expenses in order to free up some cash. Once you free up the cash, you can start paying down the debt. (Oh, and cut up your cards before you get yourself into any more trouble!) The debt-reduction strategy we're going to work through over the next few pages, called the "Crush It" system, is designed for individuals who are really squeezed for cash. It's also dead simple. Get ready. A debt-free future is within reach.

Step 1: Find a roll of wrapping paper. Yup, wrapping paper. Get your hands on some old forgotten roll that's lurking in the back of a closet. Roll out a three-foot section and tape it to your wall, coloured side in.

Step 2: Identify your debts. Now, take a marker and write down all of your debts — credit cards, loans, the $10 your buddy lent you last week — from left to right in descending interest rate order. Then, underneath each item, note the interest rate, the starting balance, and the fixed monthly payment. Let's use Mike, from above, as a working example. The table below is a breakdown of Mike's debt.

MIKE'S DEBT

	Visa	American Express	Car loan	Student line of credit
Interest rate (%)	19	18	8	6
Starting balance	8,000	9,000	5,000	8,000
Fixed monthly payment	350	300	350	200

As you put this table together, pay particular attention to the interest rate row. If you're like most people who find themselves in debt, you are more focused on the amount owing than on the interest rate. This is a common mistake. It may be more gratifying to pay off the smaller debts first, but if you're paying more interest on the larger debts, it would be wise to turn your attention to those at the outset (more on this in step 4, below).

Step 3: Negotiate your interest rates. A ten-minute phone call with your lender, in which you present a competitive interest rate offer, can save you thousands of dollars. So get on the phone and ask for a lower rate. If the lender doesn't want to co-operate, take your business elsewhere.

In Mike's case, let's assume he's successful at lowering his American Express interest rate to 10 percent (from 18 percent) and his car loan to 7 percent (from 8 percent).

Step 4: Make debt reduction part of your budget. Now the fun part starts. Every month, you need to make sure that you're in a position to make at least your fixed monthly payments, which are often preset by your lenders, though sometimes you can pay more (it depends on the terms and conditions of your debt). If you haven't done so already, integrate these fixed monthly payments right into your budget so you won't miss any. In Mike's case, he's looking at a total debt-reduction expense of $1,200 per month ($350 + $300 + $350 + $200). Put an x underneath each debt you make a payment on every month.

Step 5: Make use of your spare change. Next, you need to turn your attention to the debt with the highest interest rate. Each month, do your absolute best to put a little extra toward this debt — even as little as $20 will help.

In Mike's example, he'd want to put his extra cash toward his Visa bill. The interest rate, at 19 percent, is the highest of the bunch. A great trick to learn about extra payments is to time them so that they are made approximately two weeks after your first payment. Because of the way interest rates are calculated (especially on credit cards which is every day), you can significantly reduce the amount of time it takes to pay off your debt by breaking up the interest rate cycle! So, the more frequently you pay, the less balance the interest is calculated on.

Step 6: One down, three to go. The next step after you've paid off the highest interest-bearing debt is to pat yourself on the back and move on to the next-highest interest charger. For Mike, it's American Express. He'd go back to step 4 and do the whole thing all over again, making the regular fixed monthly payment on everything and throwing any extra money onto his American Express card two weeks after the minimum payment was due. This time, however, finding that little bit of extra cash shouldn't be as hard — after all, Mike's just freed himself from having to pay Visa every month and eliminated his car loan in the process too! Once he pays off American Express, he can repeat the same process with the next highest-interest debt, followed by the next. Remember to mark an X on your wrapping-paper table when you make your payments, and from time to time, you may want to jot down the outstanding balances so that you can see the awesome progress you're making. If you prefer to use a spreadsheet to track your debt reduction, go nuts!

That's it! It's really that simple. Below is a table showing Mike's repayment progress. Note the reduced rates on his American Express card and car loan. By going out for dinner and drinks with his friends less often each month, he manages to come up with $75 extra he can put toward his debts. As the Crush It process recommends, he applies that to his highest-interest debt, the Visa card, approximately two weeks after he makes his regular payment.

MIKE'S CRUSH IT TABLE

	Visa	American Express	Car loan	Student line of credit
Interest rate (%)	19	10	7	6
Starting balance ($)	8,000	9,000	5,000	8,000
Fixed monthly payment ($)	350	300	350	200
Year 1 ending balance ($)	4,000	6,100	1,000	6,000
Year 2 ending balance ($)	0	0	0	2,800
Year 3 ending balance ($)	0	0	0	0

This is just one example of how this method of debt reduction can work. It might take more or less time for you, depending on your unique situation. Your minimum payments may also be different. The great thing about this table, however, is that you can adapt it to suit your needs.

If, instead of using the Crush It system, you made only the regular fixed monthly payments and didn't negotiate your interest rates, it would cost you an additional $2,500 in interest charges and take over 15 months longer to pay off your debts. Check out the table below.

MIKE'S CRUSH IT TABLE

	Visa	American Express	Car loan	Student line of credit
Interest rate (%)	19	18	8	6
Starting balance ($)	8,000	9,000	5,000	8,000
Fixed monthly payment ($)	350	300	350	200
Year 1 ending balance ($)	5,000	6,800	1,000	6,000
Year 2 ending balance ($)	1,400	4,200	0	3,900
Year 3 ending Balance ($)	0	1,100	$0	1,700
Year 4 ending balance ($)	0	0	0	0

As you can see, taking your time to repay debt costs you a lot of money, and it's also a source of major stress for so many under-30s.

Ultimately, the best solution for debt reduction is to not get into debt in the first place. Or to avoid accumulating more debt while you are reducing your old debt. If you can avoid debt, you'll end up having more available cash flow. More cash for you means more options. The more options and choices you have, the more freedom you have. Keep in mind that it is super easy to spend $1,000. I could do it in a half-hour. But it is much harder to pay it back!

So what's the bottom line? The best way to avoid debt is to start living the frugal life and focus on saving for your future. By making your savings a priority, you'll be motivated enough to overcome the temptations of debt. Remember, you are saving for your financial well-being — for your own goals and dreams. In the next chapter, we're going to get specific about how to do just that.

CONSOLIDATION

If your debt situation is really, really bad you might want to consider a consolidation loan. A consolidation loan is where all your debts are wrapped into one loan at a lower interest rate, allowing you to make one monthly payment instead of three or four or more. I would highly recommend talking to your financial adviser about whether or not you might qualify. They're sometimes difficult to get, but if you don't ask, you'll never know.

The key with a consolidation loan is to not get into any additional debt while you're making payments. You don't want to take three years to pay off your loan, then have to get another one because you haven't been responsible with your money.

Sometimes debt can spiral way out of control, in which case, you may need credit counselling. In this situation, you work closely with a credit counsellor who can help you develop a plan to beat your debt and negotiate with creditors. Credit counsellors also give solid advice aimed at helping you avoid bankruptcy. A quick Google search will reveal a list of credit counselling services near you.

CHAPTER 6
Get Saving: Right Here, Right Now

Saving money is different from investing money. You save money for the things you want in the short-term — things like a vacation, new computer, bicycle, or down payment on a house or vehicle. Investing is for the long term. Think retirement.

If you're diligent about saving, you can have the things you want. And because of the short time frame, it's actually a pretty rewarding process. For example, throughout university, I saved money toward a very small down payment on a house. When I graduated, all my scrimping and saving paid off when I got to enjoy my new townhouse. The same goes for me today. I love to travel, and saving in advance for a trip is hugely rewarding. Not only do I get to travel to cool places, my credit card isn't racked up, so I can really relax and enjoy my adventure. Investing is also rewarding, but it is harder to see your end goal if your time horizon is 40 years down the road.

So, let's think about saving as something you do for things you'd like to achieve within one to three years. You might save up for a trip to Australia in two years' time by depositing money into your savings account every time you get paid. You'll earn only a little bit of interest this way, but there's no risk involved. The money that you put in will be there when you're ready to take it out.

COMMIT YOURSELF!

Many successful financial advisers suggest saving and investing at least 10 percent of everything you earn.

I think it's possible to save even more. If you are working and living on your own, why not aim for 20 percent? (I've been sticking to this goal for years now.) If you're living at home and are without expenses such as a mortgage or rent, I'd challenge you to save 50 percent. You'll never have another opportunity to save this much again. Think about what you save each month. Commit to an amount that is realistic and write it in below.

I, _____, commit to
saving and investing _____
every month.

It is important to put your savings and investing commitment above all of your other financial commitments. Remember to pay yourself first, because no one else will!

SAVING 101

Eighteen-year-old Rebecca is getting ready to head off to university in the fall. She's been attempting to save money so that she can buy a new laptop for her studies. After a few months of trying, she has given up. She just can't seem to make progress. Now school is just two months away, and if she's going to get a laptop, she's going to have to borrow some serious coin to do so.

Does Rebecca's story sound familiar? Do you have any idea what she's doing wrong? If you've read chapter 3, you know there's a strong likelihood that she's not approaching her goals in an organized way. She doesn't have a plan for action, and that's bound to lead to disappointment.

In order to successfully save, you need to have a clear sense of your goals, and a plan for getting there.

Like investing, which we'll discuss in chapters 7 and 8, saving requires some dedication. With so many tempting products on the market these days, it is difficult to save! You could easily blow $1,000 on a plane ticket in a matter of minutes — but it could take a full year to put that money back into your savings account. Yes, it's challenging *not* to give in to temptations, but the end result will be great. Down the road, you will have more money than most people your age. And that money will help you make your dreams realities.

Making It Work: The Frugal Life

Meet Aaliyah. She's a 21-year-old university student. She works a part-time job as a server at a restaurant. Luckily, her job pays well and allows her to cover tuition fees and still save a little each month. To do this, however, she has to live a pretty frugal life. She packs a lunch and buys coffee only once or twice per week. She borrows books, movies, and magazines from the library rather than buying them. She hits up second-hand stores for her clothing. Though it's tough at times, all of this frugality and saving is worth it. When Aaliyah is finished her degree, she will have about $4,000 saved up — enough for a trip or to move out of her parents' place to live on her own!

The key to being smart with your money is to live the frugal life. Now, don't panic! This doesn't mean you have to penny-pinch with absolutely everything. But it does mean that you must be conscious of what you're spending and — more importantly — *why* you're spending. If you want to get a handle on your money, get a handle on your spending!

Frugal Fundamentals

"Spend your money wisely." How many times have you heard that phrase? Was the person saying it a generation or two ahead of you? That phrase is still relevant today and has a lot of value. If you have trouble controlling your spending, try these frugal fundamentals:

- **Be ruthless.** Before you plunk down your hard-earned cash, ask yourself whether you really need the item in question, or if you just want it. If you don't need yet another pair of strappy sandals, or a new set of speakers for your stereo, then you might want to reconsider their priority on your shopping list. Having trouble sorting it out? Try waiting 24 hours before buying. Often, you'll change your mind.

- **Cut the credit.** If your credit card is getting you into trouble, hide it! Get it out of your wallet. Give it to a parent or trusted friend to hold, or stick it in a resealable bag, fill the bag with water, and put the whole package into the freezer. By the time your card has thawed, you'll have had a chance to think twice about making that "must-have" purchase — and don't bother trying to hammer away the ice; you'll just wreck the card.

- **Wheel and deal.** Everything is negotiable. If you feel your credit card interest rate is too high, call and talk about it with a customer service representative. Negotiate better rates on your debt, on your cell phone bill, on your Internet service, et cetera. Remember: if you don't ask, you don't get.

- **Pare down.** While you're in that wheeling and dealing mode, why not take a close look at your various plans. Can you live without all the bells and whistles on your mobile devices? Can you live without the absolute best downhill skis, when the average, not-so-snazzy pair will do? Think hard, and get rid of anything you don't need.

- **Become a bargain hunter.** Look for sales and discounts and use coupons when you shop. Check out eBay, auctions, garage sales, and estate sales. I've done it and had great success. For my first house, my dining room table cost $50, my TV stand was $8, my stove was $60, and my two beautiful leather couches cost a total of $500! My grand total was $618. Had I purchased these items new, I would have paid nearly $3,500. You can also check out vintage stores for cool clothes, jewellery, and accessories.

- **Entertain yourself on the cheap.** Don't forget to apply the bargain-hunting rules to other areas of your life. If you enjoy going out for dinner and to the movies, consider online group buying, keep your eyes open for coupons or "two for one" nights, or get to know the discount theatres in your neighbourhood. Better yet, why not host a potluck and movie night for your friends? Did you know that most public libraries have a great collection of old and newer movies? Yes, renting is cheaper than the theatre, but borrowing is free! You could also read more or spend more quality time with friends doing things that don't cost money, like walking or talking.

- **Think about your food habits.** We spend a ton of money on food, whether we live at home with our parents or on our own. Here are a few ideas for everyone to keep in mind:

  - If you live at home, eat at home or pack a lunch. Fast food is a budget killer and can add up to over $100,000 throughout your lifetime.
  - Stop drinking soft drink energy drinks, and expensive juices. You'll have more money and you'll be healthier.
  - Try cutting back on meat (vegetarian dishes are often cheaper to prepare).
  - Buy your food staples in bulk (the more you buy, the cheaper it gets), and fresh foods in season.
  - And, finally, trade in your "designer" coffee for a less expensive cup. (Better yet, buy a travel mug and bring your own hot beverage wherever you are going.)

- **Get healthy.** A healthy lifestyle can be remarkably affordable. Just think about it: if you drink or smoke, cutting down can put dollars back into your pocket and add years to your life.

Walking or biking instead of driving or taking public transit will leave you feeling fit both physically and financially. Why not give it a try for a week and see what kind of difference it makes?

Simple, right? Sort of. It's not easy to change your lifestyle or to cut back on things that you really like, but it's worth it in the end. Think about it this way. If you were to cut out one fancy three-dollar coffee each weekday (you could treat yourself on weekends, if you absolutely had to), you'd free up approximately $60 a month. That's $60 you could put toward your savings — for those shoes, that vacation, or a new car. It's your choice.

So, now that you've actually figured out how to free up some money, what do you do with it?

Making It Work

Meet Christopher, 17. His best friends are planning a ski trip to Whistler, B.C., in 12 months. Christopher's parents have said that he can go if — and *only* if — he pays for the trip himself. With just one year to save, Christopher is a little nervous. He doesn't even know where to start. With money, as with almost anything, the trick is to break things down into the basics. Christopher has one year to save $1,000. If you look at the year in terms of months, this means that Christopher has to tuck away about $83 per month. Because he lives at home with his parents and has very few expenses, saving that amount each month seems pretty reasonable. However, as we've already learned, saving money can be difficult. What if his car dies, or the speakers he really wants go on sale?

One way to ensure that you don't get distracted from your savings goals is to commit yourself to a plan. By following a few easy steps, you'll be able to stick to that plan and achieve your savings goals.

Step 1: Write down your goals. As we learned in chapter 1, it's much easier to stick to a plan if it's written down somewhere. In Christopher's case, he'd simply write: I want to save $1,000 for a ski vacation in one year's time.

Step 2: Do the math. Once you know what you want and when you want it, you can do some more specific number crunching. For example, if Christopher needs to save $1,000 over one year, he should put away approximately $83 a month for the next 12 months. ($1,000 / 12 months = $83 per month).

Step 3: Open a savings account. If you don't already have one, open up a savings account that has a reasonable rate of return. (You'll want to shop around to get the best interest rate). When you speak to the bank representative, make sure that the account is set up as "deposit only." This will ensure that you cannot take money out of the account using your debit/ATM card. Don't worry, when you've reached your savings goal, you can remove this designation and allow yourself to access the money so that you can purchase whatever you've worked so hard to save for.

Step 4: Automate your monthly savings contribution. Have your financial institution automatically take your savings money from your chequing account on the day you get paid. This automates your deposit so that you don't have to do it yourself. You won't forget, and you won't be tempted to spend your money elsewhere. Most importantly, you'll be paying yourself first — just like I mentioned earlier. You should be the number-one financial priority in your life ... not your creditors and certainly not a shiny new car. If you don't put aside your savings and investing funds first, no one else will.

Christopher did manage to save $1,000 in 12 months. He followed the steps outlined above and got his savings into gear. Christopher also lived pretty frugally! On food alone, he saved about $30 a week by not buying lunch every day (he allowed himself lunch out once a week, as a treat). He put his savings toward his ski trip and even had a little bit of money left over. Because he worked so hard to save his money, Christopher thoroughly enjoyed himself. He earned it!

GET AUTOMATED!

Automated banking services are handy for all sorts of reasons. Every time I get paid, my employer deposits money into my bank account. On that same day, my savings and investing money is electronically transferred from my chequing account into my savings or investment account. I also have my bills set up to be paid electronically on the day they are due. This lets me keep my money in my bank account until I must make a payment. I'm gaining interest on that amount while I wait for the due date. These electronic transfers don't take much of my time at all because I set them up ahead of time. The only thing I do is check up on my financial situation for about 10 minutes every week. Most financial institutions have online bill-payment options as well as the ability to set up automated transfers to your savings and investment accounts.

WHAT ARE YOU SAVING FOR?

When you imagine yourself one to three years down the road, what tangible things do you see? Do you own a particular vehicle or live in a certain community? Perhaps you see yourself pursuing your education. Write down some of your visions for the not-too-distant future (one to three years from now). In particular, identify some of the things for which you'd like to save.

My Savings List

- _____
- _____
- _____
- _____

Now, go back and pencil in a price beside each item you wrote down. You may have to look on the Internet to make sure you're being realistic about this.

Got it? Okay. Let's just say that the first item on your list is a car, and let's say that you're being pretty honest about the whole thing. You know that the newest BMW is not likely to be sitting in your driveway three years from now, so you're going to focus on something older and of high quality. Something you can use to get from point A to point B. Nothing fancy, just practical. Let's say you've budgeted $6,000 for this used car.

But there's also item number two. Let's say that you're expecting a medical expense of approximately $2,000 in one year's time to cover off a minor surgery. Unlike the car, which can wait a bit, you're going to need to pay your medical bill a lot quicker.

So, you know what you want. Let's do some math and figure out what it's going to take for you to get it. The key thing is to figure out how much you're going to need to save each month. You do this according to a "monthly savings formula," which looks like this:

**Purchase price / Number of months until purchase date
= Monthly savings**

For the car:

$6,000 / 36 months = $166.67 per month

For the medical expense:

$2,000 / 24 months = $83.33 per month

To pay for both things that you want, you'd need to save $250 a month ($83 + $167) for the next 24 months. At that point, you could pay your medical expense and continue saving $167 a month for the next 12 months. At the end of 36 months, you'd have enough for your car as well.

How much will you have to save each month so that you can have some of the bigger things you want? You can try this calculation with the savings items that you listed above. Just take the purchase price and divide it by the number of months in which you want to have that item. Your result will tell you how much money you need to save every month to make your goal a reality.

MY SAVINGS PLAN

Item #1: _____

_____ (purchase price) / _____ (months)

= _____ (savings per month)

Item #2: _____

_____ (purchase price) / _____ (months)

= _____ (savings per month)

Item #3: _____

_____ (purchase price) / _____ (months)

= _____ (savings per month)

How did you do? Sometimes, we find that the items we want cost more than we thought — or that it will take us much longer to save for them than we imagined. If you found that your monthly savings amount was too high for your budget, try extending the amount of time it takes to save by increasing the number of months that you put into your calculation. On the flip side, perhaps you've found that your monthly savings amount was less than you expected! If that's the case, you might be able to save more every month, and so you can shorten your time horizon by reducing the number of months used in your calculation.

One of the most rewarding experiences you can have is spending your hard-earned savings on your own goals. Enjoy your savings and enjoy your rewards!

BUMPS IN THE ROAD

Paula has been working a part-time job since she was 16. She is now 20 and has been saving her money at a rate of $150 per month for the past four years. She has about $7,200 to put toward tuition. However, when an overseas relative passed away, she needed to attend the funeral. She had no choice but to dip into her savings account for a plane ticket, a new outfit, accommodations, flowers, and meals. Now she's down about $3,000, and she's pretty much given up on her dreams of going to college for journalism for another two years.

Life brings about unexpected changes that can affect both your ability and motivation to save. However, when it comes to your financial health, you've got to roll with the punches and carry on. If you don't, you aren't going to achieve your goals. Here are a few things that you can do when unexpected events happen:

- **Recognize when your plans are getting off track.** The way to recognize this is to be organized with your money. Use tools like online banking to keep track of where it is going and why. You might be able to recognize a nasty trend before it depletes your entire savings.

- **Never give up.** Even when you are discouraged, don't give up on your financial dreams. You will never achieve them if you do.

- **Get back into your healthy financial habits.** If you've veered from a savings plan, don't wait any longer, start it up again immediately. Don't let a temporary twist in the road become permanent.

- **Be proactive, not reactive.** Try to predict, as best you can, what events will impact your finances. Then start planning for them in advance. For example, if you know you have to pay for tuition in a year, brace yourself for the expense.

EMERGENCY FUNDS

When you are getting organized with your money, I highly recommend setting up a little emergency fund — and making sure you use it only for emergencies. I broke my jaw a few years ago and needed to use my emergency funds to pay for extensive medical bills. Rather than stress about money during an already painful time — literally — I simply paid my way through the expenses — all $45,000 of them. Though I hated parting with my money, my health was at stake and you can't put a price tag on good health.

It's important that you have enough cash to carry you through things like loss of employment, emergency home repairs, vet and car repair bills, et cetera. You are the only one who can determine what amount of money you should set aside every month. I take about 5 percent of my net pay and throw it into my savings account as an emergency fund. I've found that number works well for me. Consider your own budget and how much money you will need if and when an emergency arises.

An emergency fund should be built along with your savings and investing. It shouldn't be something that you focus on purely before saving and investing. One of the keys to successful finances is balance. Balance your spending, saving, investing, emergency funds, and debt reduction.

CHAPTER 7
Get Investing, Part I: The Basics

So, you've got the motivation, the goals, and some basic financial funda-mentals under your belt. You know how to properly budget and you've identified areas in your budget where you might free up some dollars. Now it's time to get down to the nitty-gritty of investing. In this chapter, we're going to cover some investment basics — why invest, what type of investor you are, and what all those strange terms mean. In chapter 8, we'll look specifically at various investment options and strategies. Hang in for the ride because this information is valuable. It's your ticket to becoming a millionaire.

WHY SHOULD I INVEST?

What comes to mind when you hear the word "investing"? The most common response invariably has to do with money. For many of us, investing refers to the actions we take when we put money into the marketplace, a home, a stock, or a bond. But if we broaden our scope a little, we realize that the term can be used to describe many other things. You can invest in your education, for example, or invest your time in a non-profit. At its most basic, investing means that you are building your resources — whatever those may be.

You are an investor right now! You're investing in your knowledge and skills by reading this book. You're also investing your time and energy. And, as with any good investment, your efforts will pay off with increased financial knowledge and better financial health.

Just as investing means different things to different people, people choose to invest for their own personal reasons. For example, I want to invest my money for the future, when I will need it to grow my business, MeVest. I also want to invest my money for the present, like in the development and research that will give my business a competitive edge. When I think of investing any of my money, I have five primary objectives.

1. **Safety:** I want to invest my money in a way that ensures I won't lose it all.

2. **Income:** I want to use my invested money as income in the future. Though I don't need the income right now, I will down the road.

3. **Growth:** I want to grow my money using the power of compounded interest and reinvested returns.

4. **Liquidity:** I want to invest my money in things that are easy to buy and sell.

5. **Tax minimization:** I want my investments to help minimize the taxes I pay.

If you're scratching your head and wondering what the heck I'm talking about, don't worry. You're about to learn that good investments can meet all of these objectives. For now, I just want you to think about your investment goals. What do you want to achieve?

If you're still scratching your head, try flipping back to chapter 1. In the table on page 22, you wrote down some of your financial and personal goals. What were your long-term goals? Where do you want to be 10, 20, or 50 years from now? Do you want to retire at 45 and sail your yacht around the world? Own a family cottage on the shores of a northern lake? When you're considering your future — specifically, anything more than three years away — you need to shift your financial thinking from short to long term. And to achieve long-term financial success you must **invest** your money.

Over the long haul, money grows much faster if it is invested rather than simply saved. Investments offer a greater potential for a higher return. History backs me up on this. For the past 200 years, investments in things like stocks, bonds, and mutual funds have consistently outperformed the lowly savings account.

If, for example, you were to keep $1,000 in a savings account that earned 3 percent annually, starting at the age of 15 until you were 65, it would be worth approximately $4,500. If, however, you invested those funds and earned an annual return of 10 percent, which is in line with historical market returns since 1975 — so, over the past 40 years — using the annualized Standard & Poor's 500 index (a stock market index based on the market capitalizations, or value of the stock, of 500 large companies having common stock listed on the New York Stock Exchange or NASDAQ) return with dividends reinvested, it would be worth approximately $130,000 at age 65.[9] Check it out below.

Saving vs. Investing

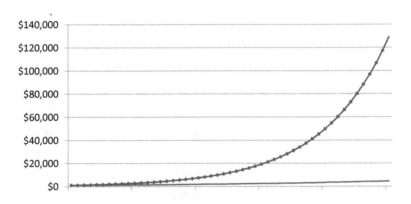

Saving your money is always better than spending it, but investing for the long term is the best idea of all.

The Power of Compounded Interest and Reinvested Returns

So, how does this work? Investing makes more money than savings over the long haul because of **compounded interest and reinvested returns**. We talked about this a bit back in chapter 1, when we were discussing the importance of time. Compounded interest is like growing your money for free. You earn interest on your initial investment. That interest is reinvested, and you end up earning interest on it as well. Now, you're earning interest on your interest. How cool is that?

The following table demonstrates the power of compounded interest and reinvested returns and it's the same example that we used in chapter 1 of this book. If you start investing your money at the age of 15, you could be a millionaire by the time you are 65 — and it takes only $100 per month to start! The best part is that to make that million, you'll need only about $61,000 of your own money. (The table assumes an average 9 percent rate of return.)

THE POWER OF INVESTING YOUR MONEY

Age	Amount Saved per month ($)	Total saved, without interest ($)	Total saved, with interest ($)
15	100	1,200	1,308.00
16	100	2,400	2,733.72
17	100	3,600	4,287.75
18	100	4,800	5,981.65
19	100	6,000	7,828.00
20	100	7,200	9,840.52
21	100	8,400	12,034.17
22	100	9,600	14,425.24
23	100	10,800	17,031.52
24	100	12,000	19,872.35
25	100	13,200	22,968.86
26	100	14,400	26,344.06
27	100	15,600	30,023.03
28	100	16,800	34,033.10
29	100	18,000	38,404.08
30	100	19,200	43,168.45

31	100	20,400	48,361.61
32	100	21,600	54,022.15
33	100	22,800	60,192.14
34	100	24,000	66,917.44
35	100	25,200	74,248.01
36	100	26,400	82,238.33
37	100	27,600	90,947.78
38	100	28,800	100,441.08
39	100	30,000	110,788.77
40	100	31,200	122,067.76
41	100	32,400	134,361.86
42	100	33,600	147,762.43
43	100	34,800	162,369.05
44	100	36,000	178,290.26
45	100	37,200	195,644.38
46	100	38,400	214,560.38
47	100	39,600	235,178.81
48	100	40,800	257,652.91
49	100	42,000	282,149.67
50	100	43,200	308,851.14
51	100	44,400	337,955.74
52	100	45,600	369,679.76
53	100	46,800	404,258.93
54	100	48,000	441,950.24
55	100	49,200	483,033.76
56	100	50,400	527,814.80
57	100	51,600	576,626.13
58	100	52,800	629,830.48
59	100	54,000	687,823.22
60	100	55,200	751,035.31
61	100	56,400	819,936.49
62	100	57,600	895,038.78
63	100	58,800	976,900.27
64	100	60,000	1,066,129.29
65	100	61,200	1,163,388.93

I know that at 15 years old it may seem tough to come up with $100 per month, but don't give up. You can get a part-time job babysitting, washing cars, or working the local summer expo. Or you can simply ask your parents and/or family members to please support your savings efforts by making contributions to your investment account instead of giving you gifts.

If you're a little later off the starting blocks, that's no worry either. You just have a little catch-up to play, meaning you'll need to increase your monthly contributions to achieve the same result. But this is manageable because you'll find that as you age, you'll start making more money and can afford to increase your investment contributions. For example, when you start working at your first job, or when you get raises or promotions, you can increase your contributions.

Just image what's possible if you doubled or tripled your monthly contributions!

No matter your current circumstances, investing *something* rather than nothing is great because you can take advantage of the power of compounded interest and reinvested returns. Remember that your greatest asset is time — the more time you give your money to grow, the better. As your financial circumstances improve, you can increase your contributions.

Stick It Out!

Sandra is 35 years old. Five years ago, she temporarily lost her job and stopped investing. She didn't have any extra income and, besides, her money wasn't growing as fast as she'd hoped it would anyway. She cashed in her investments, bought a condo and a car, and now she's kicking herself because she has zero investment money saved for her retirement. Her best friend, who kept her money invested, is watching it grow. Sandra, on the other hand, worries about the future.

Looking at the previous table, one thing becomes obvious. Unlike savings (which can take place over time periods ranging from a few months to a few years), investing is a long-term proposition. You need patience and commitment to stick to your plan. At the beginning, you may get discouraged by what seems to be a lack of progress (it takes a while for that compounded interest thing to really kick in!). If you bail, like Sandra, you'll never achieve your financial goals. If you stick with it, however, you'll start to see the results as time passes, and motivation will no longer be a problem!

Can you think of any reasons why investing over the long term might be difficult for you? Are you an impulse shopper? Do you lack the funds needed to invest? Would you rather spend on travel adventures today? To help keep yourself on track, check out the following tips.

- **Start as soon as possible.** The earlier you start, the more time you will have to grow your money with compounded interest and reinvest returns, and the sooner you'll see results. Also, investing every month will become a habit, making it easier to keep up as time passes.

- **Choose a reasonable amount of money to invest.** Strike a balance between the money you save and the money you invest. There's no point in setting your goals too high; if you fail, you'll get discouraged and you might give up. When you create your own budget, think carefully about how much you can afford to set aside. And don't worry if the amount seems small. Even $10 a month is better than nothing!

- **Automate your monthly contribution.** Have your financial institution take your monthly investment contribution straight out of your bank account on the day you get paid. That way you won't be tempted to spend your entire paycheque before you invest. Over time, you'll mentally adjust to not having this money. You won't even miss it!

- **Remind yourself that you're doing well.** While you don't want to obsess over the financial details of your life, it's not a bad idea to check in on your accounts once a month to remind yourself that you're making progress. Keep a chart on your wall or set up a spreadsheet on your computer. Being able to visualize your success will help keep you on track.

Now that you're clear on why you should be investing, you can start to think about the types of investments that might work for you. In chapter 8, we'll look carefully at the various investment options available, but before you start throwing money at the hottest stock or trendiest mutual fund, there are a few more things you need to know — starting with yourself!

INVESTOR, KNOW THYSELF!

Would you feed your fish dog food? It's doubtful. If you did, your fish (deprived of the nutrients it needs to survive) would likely end up floating at the top of its tank by the end of the week. Likewise, if you attempted to serve fish flakes to your dog, Fido wouldn't be a happy camper.

A young person's needs and desires are unique. Like the fish and the dog, each of us requires different things to satisfy our various needs. If these needs aren't met, we won't thrive. Our investment needs are no exception.

Unlike saving, which works in pretty much the same way for everyone, investing can be a highly personal undertaking. Before you dive in, it's a good idea to work up an investment plan. And before you can do that, you need to understand both your goals and your investment profile.

Investor Profiles

A happy investor is one whose investment goals and choices are properly aligned and who knows the types of investment options that will best suit his or her needs and personality. Discovering your investor profile isn't difficult. If you visit a bank with the intention of setting up an investment account, they'll likely present you with a long, drawn-out questionnaire, or ask you about a hundred questions — all designed to tell them what type of investment options would be most suitable for you. Below are some of the most common questions. If you answer them honestly, you'll have a pretty good sense of your own investment profile.

What Are Your Personal Goals?

Well! It's lucky we've already answered this one, isn't it? Refer back to chapter 1 and the discussion on goal setting. The goals you wrote down on page 22 will work just fine as an answer to this question.

What Is Your Investment Time Horizon?

This question is very important. Not all goals can be achieved with the same investment strategies. Take, for example, Rachel — a high school student who is desperately trying to save for college. Let's say that Rachel doesn't have access to student loans. Because she needs this money within a few years and because she can't afford to lose any of it, she needs to put her money into a safe investment — one that won't lose value in the short term.

Someone with a longer investment time horizon, however, would have more time during which to make up losses and enjoy gains. This person's strategy would be very different from Rachel's.

Where Will Your Money Be Coming From?

Money from a regular income is different than money given to an individual on a one-time basis. Where your money comes from, and when, can affect the type of investment you choose. Kyle, for example, works on commission and gets paid every three months. If you're in a similar situation, your cash flow is going to be different from that of someone working a regular hourly wage job. Also, commission is temperamental and can vary over time. Because Kyle's cash flow is all over the map it is important for him to work out a reasonable investment plan that fits his money schedule.

Do You Have Any Tax or Legal Concerns?

Many investors want to take advantage of tax considerations that allow them to pay less personal income tax. If this is one of your investment goals, there are a number of investments on the market that can assist. For example, investments that pay **dividends**, a small payout or reward for holding the stock, benefit from the dividend tax credit.

What Role Do You Want to Play When it Comes to Your Money?

Informing your investment adviser about how involved you want to be with your money will ensure that they understand some of your needs. Your involvement will affect the choices you make and the work your adviser has to do on your behalf.

What Is Your Risk Tolerance?

This is the big one — the most important question of all when it comes to determining your investment profile. Risk tolerance is a vital piece of the investment puzzle. In order to invest without going insane with worry or anxiety, you need to match your risk tolerance to your needs. If you don't like the idea of investments that change in value from day to day, you may not want to participate in the stock market. On the other hand, if you've got a stomach for handling the ups and downs of the market, you may want to take advantage of risky investments so that you can benefit from a higher reward in the long run. You can have some fun with the quiz below to see what type of investor you are.

1. When your math teacher comes walking up to you with a grim "you're in trouble" look on her face, you:

   a) Listen as she accuses you of something that you didn't do. You don't like confrontation and so you choose not to correct her.
   b) Say, "I'm not exactly sure what the problem is. Can you explain what's happened?" You then listen carefully to what she has to say.
   c) Deny, deny, deny.

2. Some kids down the street received new cars for their birthdays. They want to race against your dad's new sports car — a car you're normally not allowed to go near. You:

   a) Grab the keys to the shiny red roadster and kick off the neighbourhood Indy 500 in style.

b) Walk away without answering them.

c) Tell them your dad's car is worth more than all of theirs put together and that you'd rather eat dirt than face your father's wrath when he finds you with the keys in your hot little hands.

3. You're in a store where an attractive sales assistant works. He (or she) approaches you and asks if you need any help. You:

a) Tell them that you're looking for a pair of pants and say that you really like their outfit. Hey, if you find some equally trendy clothes, maybe they will ask for your number!

b) Turn beet red and say, "Thanks, but I can find my own clothes."

c) Say, "Sure, you can help me" and ask for their number when you're leaving.

4. If you were given a $1,000 bonus for doing a great job at work, what would you likely do with it?

a) Spend $400 on some new clothing. Save $500 in your investment account and donate $100 to charity.

b) Take your closest friends out for a day of snowboarding. The cost of your trip would be $1,000.

c) Stuff it all under your mattress or in your piggy bank.

5. You buy a new condominium with your hard-earned money at the age of 21. You've got a reasonable mortgage ($800/month), a great interest rate, and a roommate who pays $400 each month in rent. If you had an extra $300 a month after all your expenses, fun, and necessities were handled, you would:

a) Pool your extra money with a friend and buy another condominium that you could rent out.

b) Pay down your existing mortgage as fast as possible (you don't like to be in debt).

    c) Use half the money to fix up your condo (adding value) and put the other half toward your mutual fund investments.

Okay. Now tally your points according to the following:

1. a) 1 point b) 2 points c) 3 points

2. a) 3 points b) 1 point c) 2 points

3. a) 2 points b) 1 point c) 3 points

4. a) 2 points b) 3 points c) 1 point

5. a) 3 points b) 1 point c) 2 points

If you scored between 5 and 6 points, you're a **low-risk investor**. Your stomach will turn if you're forced into a situation outside your comfort zone. You probably aren't a huge risk taker. For example, you won't likely go cliff diving or willingly give a speech in front of a large group of people. Investing money in risky things that aren't guaranteed will not be part of your agenda. The benefit of being a non-risky investor is that you'll be very careful when you choose your *secure* investments. When the markets get rocky, you won't lose very much money. However, you won't make as much as your risk-taking counterparts over the long run.

If you scored between 7 and 11 points you're a **moderate-risk investor**. The decisions you make aren't totally wild and off the wall. They tend to be carefully planned and considered. You might be willing to venture out of your comfort zone with your investment choices, but only if they won't endanger your long-term goals. Medium-risk investments are a great fit for you because they earn a higher return than low-risk investments, with only a slightly higher risk of loss. However, you're a person who can take loss fairly well. You won't like it, but you'll pick up the pieces and move on.

If you scored between 12 and 15 points, you're a fairly **high-risk investor** and risky investment choices will suit your personality. You have the potential to make a lot of money when times are good, and to lose a lot of money when times are bad — if you don't protect yourself. If you're going to follow the risky investor route, do so with a little bit of a caution. Include some safer choices in your mix as well, and remember, there are some investment options that even professionals won't touch!

MAKING SENSE OF IT ALL

Grab a newspaper or go online to any financial newspaper, such as *The Globe and Mail* or *The Wall Street Journal*, and turn to the financial section. Are your eyes glazing over yet? At first glance, it looks incredibly boring. But it isn't. The tiny little numbers written horizontally across the stock, bond, and mutual fund pages will always state the following information. The first column tells you the name of the investment. The next tells you the volume of that particular investment traded that day. The remaining columns indicate the highest and lowest price during that particular trading day, the closing price, and the change from the previous day's price for that particular investment. If you really want things to start making sense, pick one stock — perhaps the stock of your favourite company, like Apple or Nike — and follow it daily for the next two weeks. You can track it for free online with Yahoo Finance or almost any other financial news website. These tools are typically called **portfolio trackers**.

AN INVESTMENT PRIMER: TALKING THE TALK

You're almost there. You're almost ready to take the plunge. There's only one more thing you need to know. Okay … it's more than one thing. It's several things. Dozens, maybe. As you read this chapter and the next you're going to come across a lot of weird and wacky words you may not have seen before (you may have already encountered a few that you don't fully understand). Before we start talking about bonds and stocks and the like (which will be defined in the next chapter), let's wrap our heads around some investing lingo.

- **Investment option or vehicle.** Anything (a mutual fund, stock, bond, or treasury bill, to name a few) into which you can invest your money.

- **Investment portfolio.** Your combination of investment options become your total portfolio. So, if you own three stocks and two mutual funds, they make up your total investment portfolio. A portfolio is geared specifically to your needs and investment style. It can be low risk, moderate risk, high risk, or somewhere in between, just like your investor profile.

- **Market.** A place where buyers and sellers meet to trade things of value. We buy and sell investments. The financial exchanges list the market prices for these investments online and on those newspaper pages with all the tiny little numbers. There are three major stock markets in North America: the New York Stock Exchange, the NASDAQ, and the Toronto Stock Exchange. There are also mutual fund, exchange-traded fund, and index fund markets, money markets, bond markets, and more.

- **Market cycles.** Financial markets tend to experience cycles. Sometimes they perform well, sometimes poorly. This tends to happen in waves. When the markets are performing poorly, the economy is slow. When the markets are performing well, the economy is generally strong. The five most common market cycles are:

  - **Expansion:** An upward trend. New businesses and jobs are being created and people are investing more money in the marketplace. The economy is growing and inflation is stable. This is a good time to be purchasing investments because they will grow in value throughout this cycle. Prices are also on the rise during the expansion phase of the market.

- **Peak:** Labour shortages start, wages increase significantly, demand for product is high, and interest rates are very high. Because prices have increased significantly, the market begins to react negatively. Investments like stocks and bonds tend to be very expensive. This isn't a good time to be purchasing investments, homes, cars, or other big-ticket items. They are overpriced and may lose value in the next cycle.

- **Recession or Contraction:** Economic activity begins to slow down. Unemployment rates start to rise and there is less money available in the market. Typically, it is a difficult time for people to save or invest any money whatsoever. This is an excellent time to purchase investments and other assets like houses because the prices have generally dropped.

- **Trough:** The lowest part of the market cycle. Prices have fallen substantially and so have interest rates. Consumers tend to be short on cash, but because of low interest rates, they are able to borrow money and purchase items like homes and investments at lower prices. This is the best time to purchase investments because they can be very undervalued.

- **Recovery:** An expansionary cycle during which the market starts to return to its previous peak. Many big-ticket items are purchased throughout this time and because of the increase in demand, prices start to increase again. This is a good time to be purchasing investments because the prices are still relatively low.

Markets change from year to year. Overall, however, the stock and mutual fund markets in North America have survived the ups and downs and provided an average return between 9 and 12 percent[10] over the past 40 years. Not bad.

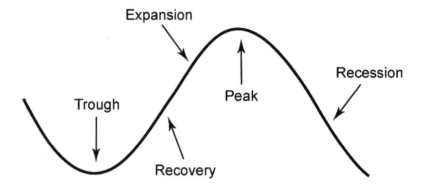

The ups and downs of the market (especially the stock market) are referred to as a "bull" or "bear" market, respectively. When we experience a bull market, the average price of stocks, bonds, and mutual funds tends to increase. During a bear market, prices decrease. Think of this as the bull market charging ahead and the bear market hibernating.

Now that you know some of the basics, it is time to start putting the pieces of this investment puzzle together. In the next chapter, we are going to learn about building your own investment portfolio. This is the exciting part!

CHAPTER 8
Get Investing, Part II: Options and Strategies

In the previous chapter you learned more about what investing is, why you should do it, and what type of investor you are. This knowledge is a powerful tool that will help you become a successful investor. In this chapter, we are going to get into some of the specific investment options and strategies that are available to you.

INVESTMENT OPTIONS

When I first started out writing and speaking about money management for young people, I had the opportunity to teach a "Dollars and Sense" course to an eighth grade class. Throughout my presentation, I used the term "investment vehicle" a number of times. Near the end of the session, I asked the class to draw a picture or write a paragraph about what they had learned throughout the day. I reviewed their work that evening and discovered numerous pictures of cars — cars on roads, cars in driveways, cars on top of mountains. Clearly, something had gotten lost in translation!

An **investment vehicle**, which I will also refer to as an investment option, is any type of investment that you use to grow your money. Your investment portfolio is made up of a number of different investment vehicles. Some investment vehicles can even hold other vehicles, kind of like a car carrier. We'll get to the details about that in a few pages, but right now let's take a look at the investment vehicles that are available to you. Knowing what they are and how they work will help you decide which options are best for you.

INVESTMENT OPTIONS

Investment type	Description
Savings account	A savings account is a regular bank account where you can safely store your money. In general, savings accounts pay very little interest and are easy to access — a drawback when trying to save for the long term.
Stock	A stock is a certificate indicating ownership in a company. These days, stocks are traded electronically, but some companies still offer paper certificates. If the company is doing well, the value of your stock increases. If the company is doing poorly, the value of your stock will likely decrease. You can make money through stocks either by receiving regular income from dividends or by selling the stock at a profit.
Bond	A bond is a certificate indicating that a company, an association, or a government has borrowed money from you. Like stocks, bonds are primarily traded electronically these days. In return for making your funds available, the bond issuer will pay you a fixed amount of interest after a fixed period of time. Rates of return fluctuate with interest rates. Some bonds, particularly those in the United States, offer a tax incentive at the time of issuance.
Treasury bill (T-bill)	A treasury bill is issued when a government borrows money from you and promises to pay it back, usually within one year. You do not gain interest on the money that you lend the government. The bill is sold to you at a discounted rate and purchased back at full value.

Guaranteed Investment Certificate (GIC) (Canada) or Certificate of Deposit (CD) (U.S.)	A GIC or CD is similar to a savings account in that it's a very safe investment vehicle (you're guaranteed to get all your money back). But, unlike with a savings account, you earn a slightly higher rate of return. Your money is typically locked away for between 1 and 5 years. To fully benefit from the predetermined interest rate (either paid out regularly or compounded), don't cash your money out early.
Mutual fund	A mutual fund is a professionally managed investment vehicle that pools money from many individuals and invests it according to a common objective. It refers to a group of stocks, bonds, or an index, which is a grouping of stocks that are tracked through what's known as an index. You and other investors purchase units of the whole, which allows you to own a little bit of many stocks. Although not guaranteed to make you money, mutual funds do provide a great opportunity to diversify your portfolio.
Index fund	An index fund is a group of stocks pulled together to represent a specific part of the market, such as the S&P 500. Money invested is not guaranteed, although the opportunity to diversify is high.
Exchange-traded fund	An exchange-traded fund is similar to an index fund, but instead of representing a specific subset of the market, it generally targets a market sector like energy or technology.

Savings Account

A savings account can be a good place to keep your money, but only in the short term. Savings accounts are considered to be "liquid," which means it's easy to get your hands on your cash. This is fine if you're using the account to store cash for things like groceries or rent, but it's not so good if you actually want to prevent yourself from spending! Also, on the plus side, because you're effectively loaning the bank your money (they invest it, after all; it doesn't just sit there in the vault!), they pay you a small — very small — amount of interest.

Perhaps the best thing about a savings account is that it's a very safe place to keep your money. In Canada, the Canada Deposit Insurance Corporation (CDIC) will insure your savings account for up to $100,000 in the event of loss or damage — if your bank goes bankrupt, for example. In the United States, the Federal Deposit Insurance Corporation (FDIC) insures savings accounts for up to $250,000. So, unlike with some of the other investment options we're going to discuss, your money is never really at risk. But you'll never achieve significant long-term growth on funds within your savings account.

Stocks

When you purchase stock, you are actually buying a piece of a corporation. You become a shareholder in that company — and you do so with the hope that the value of the corporation will increase, thereby increasing the value of your stock.

There are several ways you can make money in the stock market. You can sell your shares at a higher price than what you paid for them, you can receive a dividend (a payout to shareholders) from the corporation, or you can purchase more stock if and when the company decides to issue a new batch — this increases the size of your investment and your opportunity to earn dividends and benefit from an appreciating stock price.

The prices of shares in companies vary widely. Some sell for as little as 50 cents or lower; others go for $600 or higher. Because you need to buy stocks through some type of financial institution or brokerage, all come with a transaction fee attached. Also, unlike your average savings account, the money that you invest in stocks is never guaranteed, nor are you guaranteed any dividend payout.

Before you purchase any stock, do your research. Many people lose money on the stock market because they have absolutely no information about the company in which they are investing. Others lose money because they've received a "hot tip" from a friend who may or may not know what they are talking about. Be smart and dig around a bit. A corporation's risk level can be determined by looking into its history and by examining the direction in which the company is heading. Read the financial section of your newspaper. Go online and poke around the various investment sites.

If you know how to read a financial statement, that will also help you assess a company's value potential. If financial statements are like hieroglyphics to you, go onto *www.investopedia.com* for some help in deciphering terms like *assets, liabilities, expenses,* and *revenues.* Either way, I still recommend you consult with a financial adviser prior to making any stock purchase.

One key thing you'll want to determine from these statements is whether or not the company can afford to pay its short- and long-term debts. You can figure that out by dividing the company's current assets by its current liabilities to get the **current ratio.** The higher the current ratio, the more likely it is the company will be able to pay its bills in the short term. The general rule of thumb for many industries is that if this number is less than 1.2, the company may be in a bit of short-term financial trouble.

Another trick is to calculate a **debt to equity ratio** (divide total liabilities by total equity) to see if the company can afford to pay its debts in the long term. If this number is greater than two or three, the company may not be able to afford its debt payments over time. Again, a great tool to reference is Investopedia. You can quickly determine normal ratios for a given industry and compare your stock selection to what's normal.

Whatever you decide to do, make sure you approach stock-market investing with your eyes wide open. Even with ample research, it's possible to lose money on the stock market. Without investing, however, you're at an even greater disadvantage. That's because the stock market has typically performed better than any other type of investment in the long run. Since 1975, the stock market (measured by the S&P's 500 Index) has increased in value by approximately 2,500 percent, which on an annualized basis, without dividend reinvestment, equates to a return of 9 percent. With dividend reinvestment, that return equates 12 percent. This calculation is not adjusted for inflation.[11] So again, if you invested $1,000 in 1975 and earned a 10 percent annualized return, your investment would be worth $129,000 today. If instead you let it sit in a savings account earning 3 percent, it would be worth only $4,500 today.

If you take the time to understand how it works and which stocks are best for you, you can certainly do well investing in stocks over time. Besides reading financial books, check out these resources to beef up your investment savvy:

- *www.globeinvestor.com*

- *www.finance.yahoo.com*

- *www.morningstar.com*

Check out online articles in big papers like *The Wall Street Journal*, *The New York Times*, the *Toronto Star*, and *The Globe and Mail*.

Bonds (Fixed Income)

When a company or government needs more money than it currently has, it may look to investors (like you!) for financial support. By issuing bonds, the company or government can find the capital it needs to stay in and grow its business. A bond states that the borrower will pay a certain rate of return (interest rate) either over a specific number of years or until the bond matures.

A bond makes investors money through the interest paid out by the corporation or government to the investor. That is why these investments are often referred to as fixed-income investments. Some companies will issue a cheque every quarter (every three months) to the investor for the amount of interest they have earned throughout the period. Other types of bonds don't issue interest cheques. Rather, they wait until the bond matures and then pay the investor their principle amount plus compounded interest.

When you purchase a bond, the issuer presents you with a certificate stating the name of the company or government, the dollar amount invested, the interest rate promised, and the maturity date. Typically, as with most investments, you must be at least 18 years old to buy a bond through a broker, bank, or other financial institution. However, with the approval and support of a parent or guardian, younger investors can usually proceed with the transaction.

There are two main types of bonds: government and corporate.

- **Government bonds** tend to have secure rates of return and are sold in a variety of denominations, with the most common being $1,000. The maturity date is stated at the time of purchase, although the investor can usually cash in the bond prior to that date. A choice between compound or simple interest is often available. If you have the choice, take compounded interest — it will make a big difference to the overall value of your portfolio. Municipal bonds are another form of government bond and in some places, like in the United States, you can benefit from a tax incentive.

- **Corporate bonds** are almost identical to government bonds, although you'll likely need to put up more money to buy one. Bonds are generally considered a "safer" investment vehicle than stocks. Why? A bond is a corporation's *written legal promise* that it will repay a specified amount of money with interest after a specified amount of time. If the company happens to go bankrupt during that time, they are legally required to pay back anyone with a claim to the company's assets. No such promise exists with shareholders and stocks.

Although bonds are considered safer than stocks, there's a downside to consider as well. The rate of return on a bond can be less than the rate of return you might receive on other investment vehicles — like mutual funds or stocks. However, if a corporation in a risky financial situation issues bonds, they often have to pay a higher rate of return to their investors. There is a trade-off between risk and reward. As a general rule of thumb, safer investment vehicles pay lower rates of return whereas riskier investments pay a higher return.

Bonds are best used as long-term investments. Maturity dates tend to be anywhere from 5 to 30 years after the date of issue. When the maturity date arrives, the bond will no longer earn interest. It is ready to be reinvested or cashed in. If you want to cash your bond in early, there may be a penalty.

As with the stock market, you need to do your research before you buy. All bonds have a rating through the S&P or Moody's, which is the name of another rating agency. The Moody's rating system looks like this:

MOODY'S RATING SYSTEM

Rating	Meaning
AAA	High credit quality (the best)
AA	Very good quality
A	Good quality
BBB	Medium quality
BB	Low-medium quality
B	Poor quality
CCC	Sketchy quality (company could miss payments)
CC	Very sketchy quality (company usually misses payments)
C	Extremely sketchy quality (company has filed for bankruptcy)
D	Default (company has been forced to liquidate)
Suspended	Suspended rating (company is in serious financial trouble)

Clearly, bonds with a CCC rating are considered a riskier invest-ment than bonds with an AAA (triple-A) rating. Taking this into account, a CCC-rated bond would likely feature a very attractive interest rate. However, if the issuing company slips into a D rating, you have to wait until the legal battles are settled before you get your money back. Even then, you might not receive all that you invested. Be smart. Invest according to your risk tolerance.

Treasury Bills (T-bills)

Unlike bonds, treasury bills are short-term investments, geared toward people who want to invest their money for three to six months. A trea-sury bill is issued when a government borrows money from you and promises to pay you back, when the T-bill matures. Unlike with bonds, you do not gain interest on the money you lend. Rather, you lend your money at a discount and the government "tops you up" when the money is due to be returned. For example, you might buy a T-bill for $9,500 that is worth $10,000 on its maturity date and that's the sum you get paid. Typically you cannot get your money out of the T-bill until its maturity date.

A T-bill usually requires a large sum of money to invest — between $5,000 and $10,000 to start — making it an ideal place to stash cash for big-ticket items like cars, vacations, or down payments. The returns are moderate, but so is the risk. A T-bill can be purchased through a broker, bank, or other financial institution.

Guaranteed Investment Certificates and Certificates of Deposit

Guaranteed investment certificates (GICs) are available in Canada and certificates of deposit (CDs) are available in the United States. In both instances, they are another good low-risk investment. Typically issued by your financial institution, GICs and CDs can be purchased for a minimum investment of $500 (although some institutions allow you to buy in via weekly or monthly plans for much less). The maturity terms can be any-where from one to five years. As with bonds and T-bills, the rates of return on GICs or CDs are typically higher than what a savings account would offer but lower than many other types of investments. However, the trade-off is also the same: it's a less risky investment because it's fully guaranteed.

One of the "catches" with GICs and CDs is that your money is "locked in" until the maturity date (if you want it back earlier, there may be a penalty). Although some consider it a drawback, this feature actually makes the GIC or CD an excellent tool for individuals who are easily tempted to spend their money. It's also an ideal vehicle for investors hoping to make a big-ticket purchase within a few years.

Because GICs and CDs pay a relatively low interest rate, a young investor likely wouldn't want to keep all their money in GICs and CDs for the long term. Over the long run, stocks, bonds, mutual, index, and exchange-traded funds have outperformed GICs and CDs.

Mutual Funds

Back on page 109, we talked about investment vehicles that contain other vehicles. That's a perfect description of a mutual fund. Another analogy that often works is that of an umbrella — the mutual fund is the umbrella, under which a number of diverse stocks, bonds, or other investments are gathered.

A mutual fund is a group of stocks, bonds, or an index that a portfolio manager has chosen and crammed into a unit. The manager chooses the stocks, bonds, or investments with their clients' best interests in mind, and these investments are generally similar in terms of their risk factor. When you buy one unit of a mutual fund, you are actually buying a little bit of every investment within that unit. It is a wonderful tool for investors looking to diversify and balance their portfolios.

A mutual fund has a greater potential to make money than T-bills, bonds, GICs, and CDs, but there is also more risk involved. Since you are dealing with the stock market, you are subject to its volatility. Mutual funds follow market cycles very closely. When the markets are generally in a slump, your mutual funds are likely going to be worth less. When the markets are hot, your funds will be, too.

Mutual funds are categorized according to goals and risk levels. For example, a low-risk mutual fund would hold a grouping of low-risk stocks. There are growth funds (featuring higher-risk, higher-return investments), aggressive growth funds, international funds, income-producing funds, and many, many more.

The mutual fund market offers a solid opportunity for new investors. In fact, mutual funds were my very first introduction to the stock market at the age of 14. I used money from my job at the library to start investing in mutual funds. Unlike some other investment vehicles, mutual funds are cheap to buy into! While you may not be able to afford a significant quantity of stock or a T-bill, you can invest in the stock market through mutual funds for as little as $50 per month. Think about that for a minute. Fifty dollars a month equals two dinners out with friends. Not a big investment, and a potentially high rate of return!

Mutual funds are best used as long-term investments. Ideally, investing in mutual funds until retirement gives you ample time to grow them. However, the shortest of the "long-term" time frames is likely closer to 10 years. To receive the full benefit of a high rate of return, you must stick with your fund whether the markets are good or bad. If you hop from mutual fund to mutual fund, you end up missing out on their long-term growth potential.

MUTUAL FUND FEES

Mutual fund managers are paid a yearly management fee known as a management expense ratio (MER). Usually, this comes out of the fund itself, not out of your portfolio directly. The management fee is often a percentage of the earnings the fund makes throughout the year. It can be anywhere between 0.5 and 4 percent. Although some investors grumble about these fees, many others consider them a necessary expense. You are, in essence, paying for a service. Your fund manager is well-educated and informed — just the kind of person to help you make good investment decisions. But you'll want to compare mutual fund fees so you aren't overpaying.

Index and Exchange-Traded Funds

Somewhat like mutual funds in terms of their umbrella quality, index and exchange-traded funds allow you to buy a small piece of a large number of companies in the same industry or market. Index and exchange traded funds include ones that track the major indexes (like the Dow Jones or S&P 500) as well as ones that follow specific sectors (finance, technology, health). You can purchase these funds through your own self-managed investment account or through a financial adviser. Unlike mutual funds, index and exchange traded funds are usually managed by a computer and therefore have very limited management fees. You'll want to choose what is comfortable for you — human or computer management, or both.

Mutual, index, and exchange-traded funds are great for new investors. They're affordable, they allow for diversification within an industry, and they're not as risky as investing in stock alone. That's because you're buying many companies within one unit of the fund rather than just one company and hanging your hopes on that one company being successful.

One of the very best things about investing in index and exchange-traded funds is that you'll never underperform the market or the sector you're targeting. That is because your fund is a representation *of* the market and sector. If there's one disadvantage it's that you'll never outperform the market either.

A good strategy when purchasing index and exchange-traded funds is to look for industries (sectors) that are trending upward. For example, over the past few decades, the banking and financial services industry has consistently done well. More recently, the technology and energy sectors have exploded with new product development and the rising prices of major commodities. To succeed with index and exchange-traded funds, it is important to catch the trends and ride them like you would if you were surfing a wave. When one sector starts to slow, catch the next trend and ride it. In order to do this successfully, you need to keep current with what is going on in various industries. Beef up your business knowledge. It will pay off in the long run.

INVESTMENT STRATEGIES

Now that you know what's available to you, and a little bit about how to use it, actually building your investment portfolio is the next step to financial success. In the following pages, you'll be introduced to some key investing strategies.

The strategies presented here are not get-rich-quick schemes. Instead, they are based on sound investment advice that will carry you comfortably into your future. Sometimes you'll make money fast, other times growth will be slower. But ultimately these are proven and successful long-term strategies.

Diversify and Balance

"Don't put all your eggs in one basket!" We've all heard this one before, haven't we? In terms of investing, this phrase cautions against putting all your money in one place. After all, if you lose that one basket, you've lost everything in it! However, if you diversify with many baskets of eggs, the loss of one basket along the way won't be quite so devastating.

Another way to think about this is in terms of balance. That word — *balance* — will be a huge part of your financial life forever. It is crucial to success in investing (not to mention in your personal life!). Financially successful people learn how to balance spending, making more, saving and investing, and giving back. In chapter 7, we looked at how important it is to create a portfolio that is well suited to your investment personality. But even the most well-defined investors need to balance. Let's look at a few examples.

High-Risk Investor

Amy is comfortable taking risks. As an 18-year-old student with plenty of support from Mom and Dad, she knows she can afford to go after high-risk, high-yield investments. Amy has saved up her income from working the past three summers and has about $6,000 to invest. After lots of research and discussion with her parents, however, Amy knows that she shouldn't risk everything. She wants to have some portion of her money in secure investments just in case her aggressive investment strategy takes a turn for the worse. So she consults with a financial adviser at her local bank. After she shares what her financial goals are, they determine that she would benefit most from a combination of growth-oriented investments and a portion of more conservative, non-risky investments. In the end, Amy's investment portfolio looks like this:

AMY'S AGGRESSIVE GROWTH PORTFOLIO

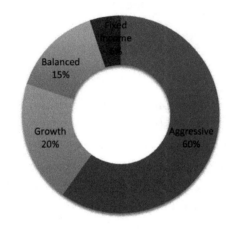

Let me take a moment to explain the labels that appear on this chart and will continue to appear throughout the rest of the chapter. Simply put, they describe a few of the investment types available for Amy's needs.

- **Cash:** Cash equivalents are investments that are very secure and very liquid (you can get your money out easily). For example, savings accounts or T-bills would be considered cash-like.

- **Fixed-Income:** These are investments that generate income by earning a set amount of interest and providing more security than a stock would. For example, a fixed-income mutual or index fund or a low-risk bond in a reputable company would suit this category (these companies have often been around for a long time and have had steady earnings over the years).

- **Balanced:** Balanced investments are riskier than fixed-income or cash investments. Often these are blue chip stocks that pay a healthy dividend or are mutual or index funds that blend low-risk stocks with highly rated bonds.

- **Growth:** These investments are even riskier. They can provide an opportunity for a high rate of return in exchange for taking a greater risk. For example, growth-oriented mutual, index, or exchange-traded funds, and stocks in companies that are well established but are in growth or expansion mode are considered growth investments.

- **Aggressive:** These are high-risk and high-reward investments, and include, for example, hot stocks, high-risk mutual or index funds, or commodity based exchange-traded funds.

Low-Risk Investor

But what if you're not like Amy? What if all that risk makes you a little nervous? Juan, on the other hand, knows that he needs to be super careful with the $3,500 he's managed to save as he heads into university and beyond. He wants to earn some rate of return, but he simply can't afford to risk what he's managed to save so far. Based on his own research, he's decided to construct a portfolio mostly around safe investment vehicles. He would therefore invest his $3,500 in a conservative portfolio. Conservative portfolios are very popular for people who must protect their money, like investors nearing retirement or a young person building a down payment for a home over the course of many years. Juan's portfolio looks like this:

JUAN'S CONSERVATIVE GROWTH PORTFOLIO

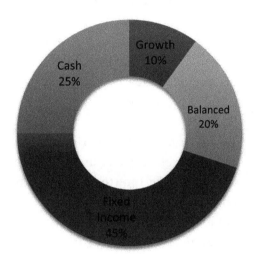

Most investors will fall somewhere between Amy and Juan on the risk scale. And that's just fine. In fact, a balanced portfolio that isn't too risky, nor too conservative, is suitable for the majority of investors. Whatever your desired rate of return, you can combine your types of investments so that they can give you that kind of return.

Thinking of investing on your own? It's not as easy as it looks. Even the pros struggle to make the right investment decisions. To be successful, you'll need access to current research (not just the news), a clear strategy (when and why to buy and sell), low fees (to make it worthwhile) and time (to carefully review your investment opportunities before pulling the trigger)

Let's look at one more example. Twenty-six-year-old Andrea has some money to invest, but she isn't sure she wants a whole lot of risk. After talking to a financial adviser at the bank, she decided to take advantage of her young age and ability to weather the market, meaning she's got more time on her side to take some risks in exchange for a reasonable rate of return. Andrea's portfolio might look something like the one below.

ANDREA'S BALANCED GROWTH PORTFOLIO

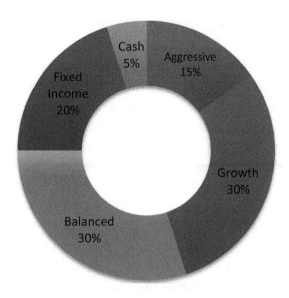

Whatever your combination, your ultimate goal is to have an investment bundle that meets your needs. Like Amy, you might be willing to tolerate a certain amount of risk. Or perhaps you're more conservative, like Juan. Or you may fall in the middle — Andrea's territory — ready to invest, but not ready to risk it all. Talk to an adviser at your local bank or financial planning institution and ask them to propose a portfolio of investments that will meet your needs. Don't be afraid to ask questions — even ones you think sound dumb. And don't forget to ask about their fees. You don't want to be forking over big bucks in fees when you're just starting out!

You have enough knowledge now to ensure that you get what you need out of the various investment options available to you. Use it!

Dollar Cost Averaging

Once you've got the diversification and balance thing down, and you've chosen the right investment vehicles for you, you can start thinking about how to maximize your investment dollars. **Dollar cost averaging** is one really neat trick. Simply defined, it means making a contribution to some type of investment plan on a regular basis. For example, you may contribute $30 a month from your paycheque. Over time, you buy $30 each month of that investment, say, a mutual fund. Due to changes in the market, the cost of that mutual fund fluctuates — sometimes the cost may be low, sometimes it may be higher. By purchasing regularly, you are taking advantage of the fund's average cost, buying more units when the cost is low and fewer when the cost is high. And regardless of the cost, you still experience the benefits of compounded interest.

Some investors think that saving up and contributing one lump sum of money will be the best way to invest. They often wait around for the prices of their desired investments to decrease so that they are cheaper to buy. All the while, they are missing out on the advantages of being in the market the entire time. It is hard to "time" the market. You don't want to be waiting around with thousands of dollars to invest, earning no return on your money.

Dollar cost averaging allows investors to be in the market at all times, taking advantage of both its highs and lows. Here's how it works. Let's say that Jason is investing in a mutual fund called XYZ. The average monthly prices are listed below. If Jason invests once per month, his average cost of buying the mutual fund is $55.91.

JASON'S MUTUAL FUND

Month	Price ($)
January	50.25
February	52.36
March	60.13
April	55.12
May	61.11
June	60.01
July	57.63
August	55.68
September	54.89
October	54.23
November	55.62
December	53.89
Average Price	**55.91**

If Jason tried to time the market and hold onto his investment dollars until he thought the time was right, he might end up paying more or less than this average. Perhaps he'd decided, after watching XYZ Fund drop in value between May and July, that it wasn't going to go any lower. Not only would he be wrong, but he'd end up paying more than the average cost of a year by buying into the fund in one lump sum rather than buying into the fund through regular monthly contributions. Investing regularly makes sense.

Always Take Free Money

If you're working for a company, you may have access to a retirement savings plan that includes a self-directed retirement savings. Often, these plans allow you to contribute a certain percentage of your pay (taken straight off your paycheque) to the plan. Some companies will even help you save money by matching a percentage of your contributions. Let's say your company agrees to match your contribution 50 percent. If you contribute $50 a month, an additional $25, or 50 percent of your contribution, will be deposited into your retirement savings plan. Your employer may not match your contributions equally, but free money is free money. Take it! Even better, your money and the money your employer has contributed will benefit from compounded interest and reinvested returns. The other benefits of employer-sponsored retirement savings programs are that your contributions are taken off your paycheque automatically — thus reducing the temptation to spend your retirement savings. Short of winning the lottery, it doesn't get any better than that!… Or maybe it does.

Besides employer-sponsored retirement savings plans, there are other non-employer retirement savings plans that are tax advantaged and will help you save even more for your future. A tax advantaged plan is registered with the government and allows you to save money on your taxes. No — the government doesn't get to meddle with your finances. Instead they simply pass along a tax benefit

In Canada, Registered Retirement Savings Plans (RRSPs) and Tax-Free Savings Accounts (TFSAs), and in the United States, 401(k)s, Individual Retirement Accounts (IRAs), and Roth IRAs are the most common retirement saving accounts. Due to higher contribution limits and associated tax advantages in the RRSPs and 401(k)s, these plans are the most popular amongst the group of tax-advantaged plans. All of these plans allow you to group different investment options — like stocks, mutual funds, or bonds — together into one plan, or portfolio. In the case of all these accounts, you save money on taxes as you build your investment portfolio.

Warren Buffett's Strategy: Prepare for the Long Haul (or Don't Buy High and Sell Low)

Looking down the road of life, what does "the long haul" mean to you? Fifty years? Forty? Thirty-five? It's worth thinking about for a moment. Here's why.

Over the past century, the North American stock markets have averaged a return of 9 to 12 percent. Many investors, however, don't reap the benefits of that excellent rate of return. Instead, they average less than a 4 percent return. Why? Investors earning 4 percent are those who keep changing and shuffling their portfolio. When the market environment changes, they get scared — buying new investments, selling old ones. Regardless of what they're doing, they're usually doing it at precisely the wrong time, probably because they're letting their emotions prevail.

Those emotions work like this. When the markets are performing poorly, the overall value of your portfolio tends to decrease. In response, you might find yourself getting a little antsy and nervous — after all, you're not making money; you may even be losing money! So, what do you do? Well, you might pull money out of your investments, thinking you'll save yourself from further losses. Actually, you're pulling out when you'll get the least amount of money for your investments. Making matters worse, you might decide to reinvest when the markets take a turn back up. Now, however, the price of investing has increased and you'll be paying more than you should.

This emotional reaction is the complete opposite of a profitable strategy. You're buying high and selling low. If you keep doing this, you're likely to make far less than average earnings and, in some cases, may not even beat the rate of inflation.

If you find yourself tempted to tamper, remember this key piece of investment knowledge: to make money with investments, you must leave your money in place for the long haul. Avoid tampering. Tampering costs you money! When your investment statements arrive, look at them quickly and then put them aside. Every year it is a really good idea to review your investments and your strategies. A lot can happen in a year and changes may cause you to alter your investment strategy. For example, if you had a baby or got married or bought a house, any of those things call for you to review whether or not your investments/strategies are still in line with the direction of your life and your goals.

Markets change and so do trends. Markets go up and down depending on a number of factors. But you have to ride the ups and downs like everyone else. Ensure that you review your strategies and keep in mind that investing for financial success is a long-term process.

Preparing for the long haul is exactly what Warren Buffett, one of the most successful investors of all time, does. He purchases high-quality investments that have the potential for long-term growth and he keeps them. His favourite sectors to purchase in are the financial, utilities, pipeline, and railroad sectors. Sound familiar? It should. Those are the same industries on those squares on the Monopoly board. I'm a big fan of Buffett's strategy and so I follow it closely with my own portfolio.

Dividend Strategies

Similar to following Buffett, I'm also a big fan of having stocks in my portfolio that pay a healthy dividend. That's because dividends are essentially free money — a reward for owning shares. Not all companies pay dividends. It's mostly those that are well established, whereas those that aren't generally need those funds to continue their growth.

In my final year of university, one of my class groups developed a dividend signalling strategy as part of a course project. We started with the assumption that a corporation's dividend policy has significant signalling implications. Some investors use dividend signalling as a way to analyze the overall health of a company. There is a substantial amount of evidence suggesting that an increase in dividends is viewed positively by the market, while a decrease is understood to be a negative signal. After all, when a company sends out a dividend, it's indicating that it has the money to do so. A dividend reduction sends the opposite message: perhaps this company is in need of cash. We wanted our mock portfolio to produce positive returns based on dividend signals.

Our strategy was to buy shares in companies that increased their dividend amounts. We held our position in firms with stable dividends. We sold a portion of our position when firms decreased their dividend amounts. Overall, our sample portfolio of 46 American companies that paid regular dividends outperformed the benchmark, which is a reference point, in our case the S&P 500, used to compare your actual performance to. We even ran the portfolio through recessionary trends. Throughout the five-year period over which we tracked our strategy, our average rate of return per year was just over 14 percent, which was a higher return than our benchmark.

Although the implementation of this strategy requires a lot of research, time, much purchasing and selling of stocks, and a significant amount of money to cover transaction fees, it is nevertheless a low-risk, stable, and fruitful investment opportunity. But you almost need to be a dedicated financial adviser to pull it off successfully.

So, if you're hoping to reap the benefits of a similar strategy, look into dividend mutual and index funds, or you could simply consider investing in stocks that pay a healthy dividend.

Be Willing to Leverage

If you had enough money available to purchase a big-ticket item, would you use it? Of course, right? Wrong. Some people actually take out loans for certain investments even when the necessary money is available. And no, those people are not crazy. Sometimes borrowing money to make money makes sense. It's called **leveraging**.

Let's say that you've saved up $5,000 for the purchase of your first used car. You've even found a really great deal on a car with all the features that you wanted. You figure you'll just pay for the car outright, but when you go to the bank to get a certified cheque, your personal banker tells you about an investment that is expected to earn 10 percent per year over a three-year period. She tries to convince you that you should invest your $5,000 in this portfolio rather than putting it all down on the car.

Now you're torn! You want to buy the car, but earning 10 percent per year on your $5,000 sounds pretty good, too. Luckily, your banker tells you that, through the use of leverage, you can do both. The bank is willing to lend you the $5,000 you need to buy your car at a reasonable interest rate of 7 percent. You'll have three years to pay back the loan. At the same time, she'll invest the $5,000 for you. Since you're earning a higher rate of return than you'll be spending on interest, you're actually making money. In fact, your overall rate of return after the three-year period is 3 percent (10 percent minus 7 percent) per year.

CALCULATING THE FUTURE VALUE OF YOUR MONEY

Are you interested in knowing how much profit you actually make if everything goes according to plan? (Remember, it's not a straight calculation of interest on the principle amount invested, because interest would be compounded annually.) A handy calculation, called the future value formula, will show you. The formula is **P x (1+i) ^ n** (P = principle invested; I = interest rate; n = investment period): principle multiplied by one plus the interest rate to the exponent of time. If your head is already swimming, don't worry. This is actually a pretty simple formula that you can plug into any spreadsheet. You don't have to do it in your head!

In the case of the car and investment scenario, this is what you need to know: The principle amount invested is $5,000. The net interest rate is 3 percent (in the world of formulas, you have to write this as 0.03 because it is a small part of one whole). The length of time over which the money is being invested is three years. In other words,

$$\$5,000 \times (1 + 0.03) \wedge 3 = \$5,464$$

This little ^ symbol means applying a power to the equation. In this equation it means calculating the equation of (1 + 0.03) three times and adding those three answers together, then multiplying that total by $5,000.

To discover how much money you actually made using this leveraging technique, just subtract the $5,000 that you borrowed from the total above. Your grand total: $464. Not bad. (If you want to get really fancy, why not consider adding a regular monthly contribution to your initial sum? You'll end up growing your money even more!)

There's one thing to watch out for when using the leverage technique. You do have to make monthly payments on the borrowed money. In the example above, you'd likely be paying close to $150 a month toward your loan. If you can afford to do this, you'll make some decent money a few years down the road.

KNOW YOUR LIMIT

A good financial strategy needs to take your personal limits into account. It is important to know when and if you have made enough (or lost enough) money. You will need to set your own personal standard so that you can be satisfied with your portfolio of investments. For example, perhaps a 20 percent return works for you. If you're fortunate enough to make a 20 percent return on a stock or another investment, you'll be ready to sell. Or perhaps you'll set your **loss limit**, how much you are willing to lose, at 20 percent. It's possible that you'll want to alter your personal limit based on changing circumstances and market conditions, but it's worthwhile to think about a starting point before you dive into investing. I'd recommend consulting a reputable financial adviser to come up with a reasonable goal for your returns.

Call in the Dogs

The Dogs of the Dow strategy was formulated in 1972. Over the past number of decades, it has proven to be very profitable for those who have followed it. The basic idea is that you purchase your investments when prices are low and sell them when prices are high. Makes sense, right? The strategy is implemented by purchasing approximately 10 stocks. The stocks you buy are the ones with the highest dividend yield at the beginning of the year. These will likely be low in price (hence the term "dogs"), because when a company pays a dividend, it is decreasing the cash it has in its business and therefore, has less value on its books. The idea here is that you purchase these stocks for "cheap" and they grow to become more valuable. Some of the best websites I have used in the past to look up information on dividends, which is what you'll need to evaluate to adopt this strategy, are *www.finance.yahoo.com* and *www.investopedia.com*.

Look for Value

With a value-investing strategy, the investor looks to invest in companies that are "beaten down" and undervalued. Understand and pay close attention to businesses that have been hit by short-term struggles. Ask this question: "Can they overcome this short-term struggle?" Oftentimes, a business that has a short-term issue can overcome it. But while it is in a pinch, you can take advantage of lower share prices. For example, during the financial crises of 2008 and 2009, many of Canada's banking stocks were hit hard, despite the excellent financial controls in place to protect both the banks and their customers. Value investors, like myself, jumped at the opportunity to invest in these high-quality institutions at discounted prices because we knew that the short-term struggles were just that — short term. Another good example would be a clothing outfitter that has felt the effects of a huge increase in demand. If it doesn't have enough inventory on hand to match the initial orders, its share price may drop in value. If it can overcome this short-term inventory struggle, the company can and will experience growth. When you are using this strategy ensure that you do your research. You'll want to invest in companies that are dealing with problems that won't significantly impact their long-term success. Newspapers, magazines, and online financial sites can be an excellent source of information about how companies are doing, including which ones are or are not experiencing success and why that is.

INVEST IN WHAT YOU KNOW

Like Warren Buffett, Peter Lynch is a famous investor who uses the "buy and hold" strategy that was described in the "Warren Buffett's Strategy" section on page 128. Lynch's key to success is his "invest in what you know" approach. With this strategy, you simply invest in companies that you know a lot about. For example, a young professional might invest in Disney, Honda, or Apple. All of these companies are instantly familiar. As well, researching things that interest you is never difficult or boring!

CHAPTER 9
Get a Job

Kai is nervous as he nears graduation from his schooling. For the past four years he's been studying environmental science and now that he's started looking for a full-time gig, his search is coming up dry. Most of the jobs in his field appear to be with the government, whose local office is in a different city. The salaries are about 30 percent lower than he expected. On top of that, there are 10 other people in his program competing for similar positions.

Getting a good job after graduation is your top priority. Second to that should be a plan to manage and eliminate your student debt by negotiating for the best interest rate, making regular monthly or biweekly payments, and paying a little extra. Third is to begin saving and investing for your exciting future. But it can be hard to find a job, given the changes in the economy after the financial crises and the increased competitiveness in the job market over the past decade.

This chapter is about making you the most competitive you can be so that you can secure a great job that pays well. But before you start firing off resumés online, it's really important to get a few job-hunting basics under your belt:

- Get a strategy.

- Breeze through the basics.

- Who you know matters.

- Your personal brand is as important as your resumé.

- Experience is everything.

GET A STRATEGY

Do you know what you'd like to do as your career? Yes — I realize you've just invested in your education to study an area you're interested in, and this question may seem a little late. But your area of study and finding something you're passionate about doing are two different things. I want to encourage you to take the next few minutes, few days, or few weeks to think hard about the career you'd like to have. Carefully consider your passions. Statistics show that people who follow their passions, while gaining practical skills, are often more satisfied with their careers and make more money than those who don't follow their passions.

If you want to be a teacher, firefighter, lawyer, or writer, jot that down in the space below. If you've got a few ideas on the go — add all of them.

My Possible Careers

- _____
- _____
- _____
- _____
- _____

When I was 17 years old and about to head off to university, I knew I was interested in teaching and also in business. I decided to get my business degree, and I knew that when I graduated I wanted to integrate my business training with educating people my age. So that's exactly what I did. I began my career as a professional speaker and wrote books and articles on personal finances for young people. But because I was just starting out as a freelancer in that field, I was paid very little. So to make more money, I also got a job as a financial analyst at an energy company, which allowed me to earn a regular income while developing my financial skills. Those financial skills in turn helped me to become a better personal finance writer and speaker.

My strategy was simple: to find a job that would allow me to make good money, and develop my financial skills while gaining more experience as a writer and speaker, essentially allowing me to pursue my passions for both business and education.

What's your strategy? Do you have a plan to integrate what you love with your educational training? What will your approach be? Is your dream job available today or will you have to work toward it? What does that time frame look like?

In many cases the right job for you may be a few years out, but finding a job today that helps to contribute practical experience to your resumé will support you in securing your dream job a little later down the road. Ideally, you'll want to spend your valuable time working on things that help you get closer to your dream job, not further away.

Sometimes, however, the types of jobs that you're looking for aren't available to you where you live. This means you may have to move. Or you may have to work for the short term at a job that you don't want to work at. In that case, rest assured, it isn't a colossal waste of your time. You'll still learn new skills wherever you go and whatever you work on. You'll also meet more people who will broaden your network — an incredibly valuable asset when it comes to the job hunt.

BREEZE THROUGH THE BASICS

If you don't have a well-written, succinct, and unique one-page resumé and one-page cover letter, get on it. A spiced-up resumé and cover letter will help you stand out from the rest of the pile. There are a gazillion different resources available to you online, like Workopolis, Salary, and Monster, to help you craft a great resumé and cover letter and look for job postings. You can also just search on Google how to write a great resumé for a new graduate.

What I can tell you is that you'll want to highlight your practical working, travel, and volunteer experiences as well as your education. That's because most employers aren't looking for top students. They're looking for top people — people who are well rounded and have had a variety of experiences that they can bring to the workplace. Yes — it's okay to highlight your school marks, but it's more important to convey that you have a variety of interests that can inform your work.

For example, as I mentioned above, my first real job out of university was as a financial analyst. I competed against more than 40 others for the same position and I won the competition. When I asked them why they hired me, my employers said it was because I was mature, had solid grades, and understood the value of hard work, as evidenced by the fact that I'd worked throughout my entire university education, volunteered for meaningful projects, like building homes with Habitat for Humanity, and was working hard to develop my skills as a financial writer. Essentially, they were pleased to see that I was well rounded and presented those facts both in my resumé and at my in-person interview.

So, what if you haven't had many extra curricular experiences? No problem. You need to sign up to volunteer for an organization you care about, join a networking group, or become a member of an organization — be it in sports or literature or whatever — that helps you build your network and develop your skills, and brings that group or organization some benefit. This will speak volumes when you go in for an interview.

Another important basic skill to have is interviewing. Interviewing can be one of the most nerve-wracking experiences for people. But it doesn't have to be. With solid preparation and by practising responses, you'll nail it.

Firstly, you'll want to have done your research on both the role and the organization that is interviewing you. Understand the requirements of the job and prepare to ask specific questions if you are unclear about job expectations. You'll also want to know what the organization is up to. What's their strategy? How do they treat their business partners and staff? What drives their decision-making? Are there recent current events that have affected their business? Much of this information can be found online, so spend some time researching. You can then weave this information into your interview in a way that makes you seem well informed and engaged in the work of the organization you're hoping to work for.

Practising responses to interview questions is also useful. Today most interviews are a blend of behavioural-type questions — "Can you tell me about a time you were in this or that situation?" — and questions regarding your practical experiences. Come prepared to share clear examples of your ability to work in a team, to pay attention to detail, to show consideration for your team and customers, and to get the job done efficiently and on time. You'll also want to be prepared to share your one- and five-year plans for your career and how you plan to develop skills that will ultimately support your long-term career aspirations.

Above all, be honest in your responses, be yourself, and pay close attention to your intuition or feelings about the job. Again, bear in mind that though it may not be your dream job, if it helps you get closer to your long-term goals, consider it a stepping stone.

WHO YOU KNOW MATTERS

I applied for a job in government relations and communications about six years ago. It was a great fit all around — blending finance with writing and public policy. I went for multiple interviews and nailed each one. I even received positive feedback from the hiring manager. I waited and waited for weeks on end while they made their decision. Finally I heard back that I had been unsuccessful in getting the job, but that I was the second runner-up. I was super disappointed and quite confused, given the positive feedback I'd received during the process. A few months later I learned that the successful candidate was the son of one of the vice-president's best friends, who worked there.

What the heck?

I learned a really valuable lesson at the time — my resumé wasn't the only thing up for consideration; my network — the people I know — was as well.

Do you have a broad network? Do you know how to lean on your network for support?

When you're starting out with your job search it is incredibly important to spend time developing your network. That means having coffee, lunches, and "get-to-know-you-better" chats with people who have jobs you aspire to have or are leaders in the industry you're interested in and who may want to hire you. If you spend time developing these relationships, and communicating what you're about and what kind of work you're looking for, you can lean on your network to open up further contacts, refer you to job posting, and even provide you with advice.

To build a network you need to be strategic — just like in this job-hunting process. Who in your circle of friends or family members has a job you're interested in or has other good connections? Reach out and take them for coffee. While you're there, run through the following:

- Tell them you're looking for work.

- Find out more about what they do.

- Inquire if they know of anyone looking for a candidate like you.

- Ask for a few tips or words of wisdom for your search.

- Ask them to put you in touch with a few more people who could give you advice regarding your career hunt.

- Find out if they, or someone they know, might want to be a mentor to you. A mentor can provide you with helpful advice about your career path, tell you what mistakes to avoid, open up their network, and wants to watch you grow and succeed. They are generally in a field of work that is similar to your own, but they don't have to be.

Whatever you do, don't forget to send over a thank-you card or email or give them a thank-you phone call.

Courtesy matters while you're building up your contact list, and no one wants to refer a person who lacks basic manners or is a jerk.

YOUR PERSONAL BRAND IS AS IMPORTANT AS YOUR RESUMÉ

You've probably heard about this **personal brand** thing before — it's essentially what you're known for and how people perceive you. For example, I work really hard on my personal brand so that people know I'm the go-to-gal (who's young) for personal finances for young people in North America. They know I'm also the owner of MeVest — a company that's dedicated to helping young people reach their financial potential through fun online resources.

Your personal brand is built through your reputation, and we all know how reputations are built — through perceptions of you, the people you know, and what you've done. These days your social media activities also contribute to your personal brand and WILL affect your job search. So, if you've got oodles of pictures online of you shotgunning beers, you might get a reputation as a party animal. If, on the other hand, you become known through word of mouth in your community for being a great volunteer who knows how to help others while having fun in the process, you'll attract better employment opportunities.

When you think about your personal brand, think about what you want to be known for — your hard work, good communication, innovation, or being a great driver, an excellent swimmer, or everyone's favourite server. Ideally, you want your brand to be a positive reflection of yourself today and what you're capable of in the future.

Now, you'll need to build up support that indicates that you actually are what you say you are. This means having a social media presence that reinforces your brand. It also means lining up your references so that they say the same things about you. It even goes so far as ensuring that your personal network talks about you in the same way.

The only way this is going to happen is if you behave in a way that reflects what you say you are. When you do things that are inconsistent with your personal brand, you're going to confuse people — especially employers who are looking to see that you have consistency of character and are who you say you are.

So take down those ridiculous photos from your social media accounts. Draft up some talking points about who you are and what you aspire to. Give your network the same message. And do what you say you're going to do, every day.

The stronger your personal brand, the more likely it is you'll have great job success.

EXPERIENCE IS EVERYTHING

I know how hard it is to gain experience when the job market is so tough. Take any opportunity to build up practical experience that is directly related to the work you want to be doing. One of the best ways to do this is to apply for internships (paid or unpaid) or to volunteer for an organization that requires your skill set, and immerse yourself in the business you want to be in, even if it's not the right job. A great example of this is my good pal Corinna, who was in university, working during her summers off from school as an administrative assistant at a brokerage firm. When she completed her degree in economics, she got hired on full-time as a trainee investment adviser by that same company. Her administrative work with the company had little to do with her role as an investment adviser, but she'd learned some basic principles of the business while in her summer role. She'd also been able to expand her network and get a top investment adviser to mentor her while she was there.

If you're having trouble finding a job that's related to your field of study, you'll need to broaden your horizon. For example, if you're hoping to become a health and wellness writer, you may want to consider a sales job in medical supplies while you're continuing your search for what you truly want to do. The idea here is that gaining some experience is better than having none. Your experiences will help you to build your network, develop your skills, prove to others what you're all about, and develop your personal brand.

THE NON-TRADITIONAL JOB

Making money helps you reach your goals of becoming financially successful. Traditionally, we think about working a regular job as a means to make money. However, you can think about making money in a variety of entrepreneurial ways as well. If you've got a great idea, you could develop a solid business plan and start your own business. Or you could simply try to spruce up your income through buying and selling things online, babysitting, house-sitting, dog-sitting, tutoring, or freelancing other services.

A non-traditional job typically requires a lot of creativity, so put your thinking cap on. Isn't that what every young tech billionaire had to do to get started?

IT'S NOT ALL ABOUT PAY

Selecting a job should never be driven solely by what that job pays. That's how people end up selling their souls to their employers! You'll want to strike a balance between doing what you're passionate about and earning a respectable income. If you're like me when I was starting out, you may need to supplement your income with a part-time job or by freelancing. Over time, as you grow your skills, you'll begin to earn more.

Now — on the flip side — I am not a proponent of earning less than you're worth. So understand your market value, fight hard for your pay through regular reviews and such, and don't be afraid to ask for what you want. So long as it's reasonable, you and your employer can work toward it. But more money typically means more responsibility, so be prepared to roll up your sleeves.

Finding the right job can take time so don't get overwhelmed or disappointed if you don't find the right thing straight out of the gate. Carry on and be patient with the process. But do not delay networking. You must pound the pavement hard to develop your connections so that they can help open doors for you.

CHAPTER 10
Get Specific: Homes, Kids, and Stuff Like That

This chapter deals with specific situations that may or may not apply to you yet. However, at some point in your life, these things (education, house hunting, retirement, having children) might be very relevant. For example, if you are 16 and in high school, you might not be thinking about kids or houses just yet. However, if you are nearing the end of your college years, you might be considering purchasing a home or marrying your honey. If you are married or engaged and thinking about children, you might be interested in saving for your children's education. Regardless of these scenarios, one thing remains true: Everyone in any life situation should be thinking about their financial future and retirement. Though it seems very far away at the moment, it's not. Retirement is inevitable and has a way of creeping up on even the youngest people.

EDUCATION

Marla wants to go to university to become a teacher. She is aware that her education costs will add up to approximately $15,000 per year, which includes living expenses. Unfortunately, her parents are not in a position to help her out with the cost of her education. Although Marla has heard horror stories about student loans, she's beginning to wonder if they might be the only answer to her dilemma.

Most financial books don't include strategies designed to help pay for education — but then again, most investment books aren't written for people under 30! But what if, like Marla, you're facing the challenge of paying for your own education? You are not alone. Only a handful of people are lucky enough to go to school debt-free. Most students rely on lines of credit or student loans to get through, and the majority of students in North America graduate with between $20,000 and $30,000 in student debt.

If you know in advance that you will have to pay for your own education, you might want to consider a **stacked GIC or CD** strategy. Back in chapter 8, we learned that GICs and CDs guarantee you safety and some interest while they are invested for a specified period of time. GICs are available in Canada and CDs are available in the United States. Both are each other's equivalent. Most importantly, GICs and CDs have different maturity dates and you can choose when you want them to mature. A stacked GIC or CD strategy is sort of like a forced savings plan. It involves investing in GICs or CDs before going to school and throughout school. With proper planning, you can ensure that one GIC or CD will mature every year throughout your post-secondary school career — effectively releasing a handy sum of money that will assist you in paying for tuition and books.

Let's use Marla, from the case study above, to show us how this can work. In the summer between grades 10 and 11, Marla gets a part-time job at a golf course. Since she's working full-time hours throughout July and August, she manages to make about $3,000. Because she's still living at home with Mom and Dad — who pay the mortgage, the bills, and for all of her food — Marla manages to save $2,000 from her earnings. At the end of the summer, she visits the bank, speaks to a financial adviser, and purchases a GIC/CD with a decent rate of return and a two-year term, meaning that it will mature during her first year of teachers' college.

The following summer, between grades 11 and 12, Marla works at the same job and again manages to save $2,000. Once again, she visits the bank at the end of August and purchases another two-year GIC/CD with a decent rate of return. This means that when she's about to start her second year of teachers' college, her second GIC/CD will mature.

See? If Marla continued with this pattern of saving and investing in a GIC/CD every summer, she'd end up "stacking" her GICs/CDs (see the table below) so that one matured at the beginning of each year of teachers' college.

MARLA'S GIC/CD INVESTMENT STRATEGY

	Year 1	Year 2	Year 3	Year 4	Year 5
Original Investment in GIC/CD ($)	2,000	2,000	2,000	2,000	2,000
Interest Rate (%)	3	3	3	3	3
Value at Maturity ($)	2,120	2,120	2,120	2,120	2,120
Investment term (years)	2	2	2	2	2

I know, I know! First-hand experience has certainly taught me that $2,120 isn't enough to pay for a full year of college education, but it is $2,120 more than you'd have if you didn't invest at all, and it certainly puts a dent into those tuition costs! Think about it this way, Marla will have put $10,600 toward her tuition throughout her schooling by following this strategy. She will ultimately have a much smaller student loan balance upon graduation by paying for some of it herself.

Another thing to note: When Marla starts university, she can take advantage of the fact that she has an extra two months to work each summer. She can earn more, and save more in her GIC/CDs. A good deal all around!

HOME SWEET HOME

Krista is a 24-year-old new graduate and she wants to move out of her suburban family home as soon as she can. She has her heart set on a condo near the city centre — close to her friends and potential employment prospects. But she is currently paying off her student loans and is wondering how she will ever afford a down payment.

Over the past 25 years, the North American condo market has exploded and developers are targeting under-30s as their primary buyers. Why? Condos are typically less expensive than detached homes. They are easy to care for and manage. They also offer young people a perfect way to enter the real estate market, without being left completely strapped for cash after making a down payment.

First-time homebuyers face significant challenges when they enter the real estate market. Not only do you need to come up with a down payment in order to buy, but homes — whether a townhome, condo, or detached house — also require a mortgage, unless you have oodles of savings or you're lucky enough to have your parents give you the money to buy the house outright. A mortgage is a long-term debt instrument used to pay for your home. It is like having a contract stating that a certain property, your home, will be pledged as security against the value of the loan. So, if you don't make your payments, the bank will take your house. Mortgages often take 25 years to pay off. This may sound scary, but a mortgage is, in fact, very beneficial in the long run. Homeowners are nearly 30 times wealthier than people who rent their entire lives. Purchasing a home, rather than paying money in rent each month, can be an excellent long-term investment. But the costs of owning a home can also be high and need to be balanced so that you don't end up being able to afford only your home and nothing else. It's really important to note that one of the largest challenges with the real estate market in recent years has been its volatility. When the markets were thriving, pre-financial crises, home values increased rapidly. When the market crashed, many North Americans were left with mortgages that were worth more than the value of their house. This is why so many homes were foreclosed upon — that and the fact that so many people lost their jobs and couldn't afford to pay their mortgages. Since that time, things seem to have settled down, but it's still very important to be aware that an overheated real estate market often ends, and in many cases, at the expense of homeowners.

So, how do you go about saving a down payment? Well, you could start socking away money for that down payment in your chequing account or hide your cash in a safety deposit box until you are ready to make the purchase. But by this point you know that these approaches aren't going to get you very far. Sure, you might gain some interest over the years, but you might also dip into your savings from time to time. All in all, these are terrible ways to save your money for a long-term, big-ticket item.

Remember Krista, from earlier? Well, she is actually in pretty good shape. She has three things going for her: she has a well-paying job as a safety coordinator, she knows what she wants, and she's willing to figure out a way to make it happen. Because she has some time on her side to save — three to five years — she'll want to ensure that she's earning interest on the money she invests, and she'll want to make sure that she can't touch that money (and accidentally ruin her long-term dreams because of one fabulous pair of shoes!). It wouldn't hurt, either, for Krista to look for ways that she can grow her down payment while in the savings process.

The very first thing Krista needs to do is visit her financial institution. Taking into account local laws, interest rates, and her personal financial situation, an adviser will be able to determine how much money she needs to save in order to cover a down payment. The typical minimum down payment is 10 percent of the value of the house. So if a house costs $200,000, a 10 percent down payment would be approximately $20,000. That calculation looks like this:

$$\textbf{\$200,000 x 0.10 = \$20,000}$$

In Krista's scenario, let's assume that she takes either three, four, or five years to save the money to make a down payment on a home. Let's also assume that she is choosing to save between 10, 15, or 20 percent of the value of the house. Have a look at the table below to find out how much money she will have to save every month in any of these scenarios.

MONTHLY SAVINGS FOR A DOWN PAYMENT

	10%, or $20,000	15%, or $30,000	20%, or $40,000
36 months (3 years)	$556	$833	$1,111
48 months (4 years)	$417	$625	$833
60 months (5 years)	$333	$500	$667

But what if Krista starts saving her money in a high-interest savings account with compounded interest or a GIC or CD with compounded interest? Both of those investments are very safe and secure, so Krista won't have to worry that she's putting her down payment at risk. She could also explore a money-market mutual fund. Though they don't guarantee that her money is protected, they are considered extremely safe investments because they are invested in the safest, most secure securities, like short-term government bonds. Krista can expect a reasonable rate of return. And she'll reach her goal faster by earning interest on her growing investment. She should shop around for the most competitive interest rates, while choosing the safest investment in the process.

Let's assume that Krista decides to save for a 10 percent down payment of $20,000 over the course of three, four, or five years, with an investment rate of return of 3 percent. Here's what her savings will be worth at the end of each year:

MONTHLY SAVINGS TOWARD A 10% DOWN PAYMENT ON A $200,000 HOME

	36 months (3 years)	48 months (4 years)	60 months (5 years)
Monthly savings ($)	556	417	333
*Year 1 ($)	6,800	5,100	4,100
*Year 2 ($)	13,800	10,300	8,300
*Year 3 ($)	21,000	15,700	12,600
*Year 4 ($)		21,300	17,000
*Year 5 ($)			21,600

*Values have been rounded to the nearest hundred dollars.

As you can see, time is on Krista's side. If she takes less time she'll have to save more money each month, but she will be able to purchase her home sooner; if she spreads out saving longer, she'll have to save less each month, and won't be able to purchase her home for a few more years. But she'll earn more interest. She'll want to choose a time frame that suits her budget so that she can afford to make regular contributions to her down-payment fund while balancing the repayment of her student loans. Krista will also want to prepare herself for the closing costs of a future real estate transaction, which can be anywhere from 1 to 3 percent of the purchase price of the home. So she'll need to save for a few months longer than in her original plans. Regardless, with a little forethought, planning, and sticking to a budget, she should have no trouble making her dream a reality!

Getting Aggressive: The Possibility of Leveraging

If you are fortunate enough to have saved a solid down payment for a house, and have already found your dream home, you should take a very aggressive approach to your next house-buying step: mortgage-rate shopping.

As with any other purchase, you want to be very certain that you are getting the best value for your dollar. When it comes to mortgage rates, even 0.5 of a percent can make a huge difference in your monthly mortgage payments. Below is a table with monthly mortgage payments rounded to the nearest dollar for a 25-year amortization period — the length of time it will take to pay off the full loan.

MONTHLY MORTGAGE PAYMENTS AT VARIOUS VALUES AND RATES

	Mortgage Amount				
	$100,000	$150,000	$200,000	$250,000	$300,000
Interest rate (%)	(monthly payment)	(monthly payment)	(monthly payment)	(monthly payment)	(monthly payment)
3	473	710	946	1,183	1,420
4	526	789	1,052	1,315	1,578
5	582	872	1,163	1,454	1,745
6	640	960	1,280	1,600	1,919
7	700	1,051	1,401	1,751	2,101

The table clearly shows that the lower your interest rate, the more you'll save on your mortgage. So fight hard for the best rate with the greatest flexibility.

It is also important to consider the power of leveraging (see chapter 8) when you're about to purchase a home. Paul has been very lucky. Thanks to a sizable gift from his grandmother and some hard work at two jobs — bartending during the summer and teaching grade school throughout the school year — Paul has managed to save $60,000 toward a down payment. The condominium he's set his sights on costs $120,000. The bank has already told Paul that he needs to put down only 10 percent, or $12,000, in order to secure the unit he wants. Paul knows that the more he puts down, the lower his monthly payments will be. However, Paul is reluctant to part with all of his hard-earned money. Therefore, he's weighing the pros and cons of putting down only 10 percent of the home's value — $12,000 — versus 50 percent of the home's value, which would be his entire savings of $60,000.

Before he makes any hard and fast decisions, Paul should take a good look at the interest rate the bank is offering. Again, if Paul's credit score is healthy, his interest rate will be very low compared to the interest rate offered to someone with a low score. A higher rate of interest can add up to thousands of dollars in extra interest, so lower is always better.

If Paul is offered a competitive and low mortgage rate, he might want to consider making his down payment as small as possible so that he can use his remaining savings to invest and hopefully earn a higher rate of return through the power of compounded interest and reinvested returns than the rate he would pay on his mortgage.

Let's crunch some numbers and see how this works. Remember, Paul has saved $60,000, the condo costs $120,000, and the bank is asking for a $12,000 down payment. If he put only $12,000 down, he would be left with a mortgage of $108,000, and $48,000 to invest elsewhere (for simplicity's sake, we're going to leave closing costs, mortgage insurance, and other financing fees out of the equation here).

Let's say that Paul and his financial adviser find an investment portfolio that is expected, not guaranteed, to return 8 percent annually. Remember the time value of money formula (see chapter 7):

$$P \times (1 + i) \wedge n$$

P = principle invested; I = interest rate; n = investment period

In Paul's case, the formula works out like this:

$$\$48{,}000 \times (1 + 0.08) \wedge 1 = \$51{,}840$$

What this means is that Paul would invest his $48,000 into that investment vehicle and in one year's time he will have earned $3,840 in returns ($51,840 – $48,000). He can now use that $3,840 to help pay off his mortgage or he can reinvest that money back into his investment portfolio and grow his money even more.

The basic idea is this: If Paul can take advantage of a low interest rate on his mortgage — lower than what he expects to make on his investments (8%) — he will come out on top. For example, if he is paying 5 percent on his mortgage and making 8 percent on his investment portfolio, then theoretically he is ahead by 3 percent (8 - 5 = 3). Therefore, it is in his best interest to put additional money on the mortgage, seeing as he is making less on his investment portfolio.

The risk in this scenario is that if the markets are performing quite poorly, Paul might end up making less than 8 percent on his portfolio in the short run. If his rate of return on his investment portfolio is 4 percent and his mortgage rate remains at 5 percent, he is paying a greater amount of interest on his mortgage, so he would be financially behind in that scenario.

There are a number of factors playing into Paul's scenarios, for example, the value of homes in certain areas, expected market performance, and Paul's risk tolerance toward debt. He should consult with a financial adviser before pursuing this strategy, and so should you.

There are a variety of mortgage structures from which you can choose, including open (flexible) to fixed (non-flexible). Some offer payment options like weekly, monthly, or biweekly accelerated payments, and many allow you to prepay a certain amount of the mortgage each year without penalties. It is really important to review these options and select a mortgage that is the right fit for you.

RETIREMENT SAVINGS

There are a variety of tax-advantaged retirement savings plans that allow you to save money for the long term, including your eventual retirement. And if you think this stuff sounds way too far off to be worried about, remember chapter 1. If you don't care about and invest in your own future, who will? Waiting to win the lottery or inherit the family fortune is not a viable financial plan! And don't forget, the earlier you start, the better off you'll be through the power of compounded interest and reinvested returns.

As mentioned in the previous chapter, the two most common tax-advantaged plans in Canada are Registered Retirement Savings Plans

(RRSPs) and Tax-Free Savings Accounts (TFSAs). In the United States, comparable plans are the 401(k), 403(b), IRA, and Roth IRA.

It's helpful to think of a tax-advantaged plan as a house — a house that needs to be decorated. An investor can fill that house with the types of "decorations" (investments) he or she wants — mutual funds, stocks, index funds, and more (remember chapter 8). As with a real house, the decorations are chosen according to the tastes and needs of the owner — in your case, they need to suit your investment personality. Some people like flashy, risky things; others go for classic, conservative styles; others still might prefer a mix. Whatever your taste, a tax-advantaged retirement savings plan allows you to create a balanced portfolio that suits your needs and investment style.

Why bother with a tax-advantaged retirement savings plan? Why not just invest in each component separately? Good question. The answer lies back with that investment strategy outlined in chapter 8 — the one about always taking free money. When you set up and invest in a tax-advantaged plan, the dollars you invest with are taxed at a lower rate, so that means you pay way less to the taxman and keep more for your investment portfolio. The other thing to note is that most employers offer tax-advantaged retirement savings plans that allow you to pick the investments that go into the plans, and they may also match a portion of your savings.

There are limits on the amount of money you can invest in tax-advantaged plans, but don't worry, they are sizable and shouldn't be a barrier to you starting to contribute to your plan. Now, don't go getting all excited! This doesn't mean that you never pay taxes on the amount you invest. Depending on the plan, you'll either pay taxes when you retire (but usually at a lower tax bracket, because you'll be retired and earning less) or before you invest — essentially you invest with after-tax dollars; the net amount paid into your bank account. The amount of money you save on taxes varies depending on your income level, associated tax rate, and how much you contribute to your tax-advantaged plan.

So, when should you start investing? Is it ever really too early to start thinking about retirement? Not really. Typically, people start investing in retirement savings plans when they get their first full-time job. However, nowadays, you can set these types of plans up even while working a part-time job. The easiest way to make retirement saving painless is to time your contributions to coincide with your paycheque. So, if you get paid once per month, ensure that you contribute to your plan on that day. Similarly, if you get paid biweekly (every two weeks), set your contributions to match those days. Automating your contributions is a terrific idea — you won't have to worry about manually writing cheques, making your own bank transfers, and/or visiting your financial institution every time you get paid.

Most retirement savings plans can be established with as little as $25 per month. But as your income and lifestyle change, adjust your contributions accordingly. Here are my top three tips for retirement saving:

- Increase the size of your contribution when you get a raise. This totally makes sense because when you get a raise, you end up paying more in taxes. To counter that, a tax-advantaged savings plan will help you save on your taxes. If you set your contribution as a percentage of your earnings rather than as a set amount, you'll automatically increase your contributions when you get a raise.

- Match your risk tolerance with the investments you choose for your tax-advantaged savings plan. As you get older, you'll want to decrease your exposure to risk by choosing less risky investments, because you'll have more to protect, like a home or family. Or you might be nearing retirement and not have as much time to recoup losses.

- Maximize the benefits of any employer-sponsored retirement savings programs. Again, that's because employers will contribute to your RRSPs. So take advantage of free money! Just think — if you invest in an employer-sponsored plan where you put in $1,000 and your employer puts in $500, you'll have a total of $1,500 invested. Your colleagues who don't invest using that plan would have to come up with all $1,500 on their own to achieve the same result.

BORROWING TO INVEST?

An investment loan for your tax-advantaged retirement savings can be a wonderful thing, but only if you can afford it. This type of loan is designed for people without available savings who want to contribute to their retirement savings plan in a particular tax year to maximize the tax credits available to them for that year. Oftentimes these loans have very reasonable interest rates and can be paid off within a year or two. It really only makes sense to take out an investment loan if the taxable benefit received from the contribution is greater than the amount of interest that will have to be paid on the loan. I'd recommend bargaining for the best interest rate possible, doing the math, and ensuring that you can indeed afford to make the monthly payments.

Saving for Your Kids' Education

The cost of education has increased by more than 100 percent since the 1980s, making it difficult for a parent, grandparent, or guardian to save enough. Thankfully, governments in North America offer unique plans to help you save for your child's future education costs, including the cost of tuition, books, and the like at most accredited trade, university, and college programs. In Canada, this program is the Registered Education Savings Plan (RESP), and in the United States, the most popular plan is the 529 plan. In both cases, the government helps you save by either providing a grant that matches a portion of your contributions or reduces the amount of money you are taxed on contributions you make. There are limits in each country as to how much you can contribute to these plans — sometimes annually and other times throughout the life of the plan, but contribution limits are sizable.

To set up an RESP or 529 plan you'll need to fill out some paperwork at your local bank, have a Social Insurance Number or Social Security

Number for your child, and then you'll need to select the types of investments to go into the plan. Again, these investments should be suited to your risk tolerance.

If your child decides not to go to school, the money you've invested and the interest it has earned still belong to the child. The government money (and any interest it has earned) goes back to the government.

Conclusion

You've embarked on an awesome journey — a journey to better your financial knowledge. You now know more about investments and basic finance, and the tools that will help you achieve your financial dreams, than you did when you picked up this book. You are well equipped to become "rich by 30"!

But always remember that becoming rich by 30 isn't only about money. It's about striking a balance between your financial, personal, and career life so that you can achieve your full potential.

Still, you may find yourself wondering where you go from here. You aren't alone. It's completely normal to be overwhelmed by so much information. If you find your head spinning, or if you're worried about losing your focus, concentrate on the following 10 pieces of advice. They'll ensure that you stay the course.

TEN PIECES OF ADVICE

1. **Start now.** Whatever your financial situation may be, start to invest right now. Time is of the essence. The longer you wait, the less wealthy you'll become. Think of it like this: by waiting, you are actually cheating yourself out of money. Start investing when you are young. You'll thank yourself later on.

2. **Get educated.** This is the most lucrative investment you're going to make in your lifetime and it's 100 percent guaranteed, because no one can take your education away from you.

3. **Get smart after graduation.** Push hard for a good job that pays well after you graduate. Work hard. Develop your skills. Communicate your successes and fight for regular salary increases. If a regular nine to five doesn't work for you, try your hand at entrepreneurship.

4. **If you don't need it, don't buy it.** Overspending can have an incredibly negative influence on your life. Couples that have spending problems, for example, are typically the first in line for a divorce. Overspending can spiral into debt and bankruptcy — and that affects every area of your life. You can control your spending through effective budgeting and examination of your priorities. It just requires a change in your mindset.

5. **It doesn't matter what you have, it's what you do with it that counts.** You could be the poorest person on the block. You might have only $25 to save each month. You might have only $10! It doesn't matter. Do it! Don't be discouraged. There are thousands of very wealthy people who started with almost nothing. You can do it, too!

6. **Contribute regularly.** By contributing to your investment portfolio regularly, you get to take advantage of the average price over the long haul. You don't have to worry about timing the market. Leave that to the experts.

7. **Diversify.** If you have all of your eggs in one basket, and you drop that basket, all of your eggs are going to break. Diversify your investments to reduce your risks.

8. **Be patient.** Money grows exponentially over the long run. It doesn't necessarily grow immediately. Hang on for the ride. Markets change so much through time. They go up and they go down. Try to see past the short-term fluctuations and focus on the long term. In the past, over the long term the markets performed a return of 9 to 12 percent. Investors who focus on the short term have made only about 4 percent. Figure out a strategy that suits your risk tolerance level, and stick with it through thick and thin.

9. **Pay yourself first.** You need to balance your debt reduction with saving and investing. Don't concentrate on one area and ignore the other. Use the "Crush-It" technique outlined in chapter 5 to get rid of the debt that's holding you back, but always ensure that you are saving some money as well. Saving for your future should be the top priority in your personal budget.

10. **Strike a balance.** Rich people do four things better than the average person — they spend wisely, make more money, save and invest for the future, and give back to their communities. This last thing can be achieved by volunteering or by donating funds or goods to a charity. You'll feel good knowing that you've done something positive for the community and for yourself.

You can refer back to these pages whenever you need a refresher course or just a little motivation. I also recommend that you further enrich your knowledge of money management by continuing to learn and practise healthy money-management techniques. Check out my website, *www.lesleyscorgie.com*, and my company website, *www.mevest.ca*, for more information and access to my online eLearning platform for financial literacy. Or follow me on Twitter at @LesleyScorgie for regular financial tips and answers to your questions.

Now get out there and get going! Good luck!

Notes

1. The U.S. Department of Labor and Census Bureau conducted a study in 2004 that suggested 75 percent of future North American jobs will require some type of post-secondary education. Additionally, they found that jobs requiring a bachelor's degree would grow twice as fast as the average for other occupations.

2. Robert Longley, "Lifetime Earnings Soar with Education: Master's Degree Worth $2.5 Million Income Over a Lifetime," updated August 17, 2013, U.S. Government Info, *usgovinfo.about.com.*

3. Two references were consulted. Statistics Canada, "Education and Occupation of High-Income Canadians," *www.statcan.gc.ca.*

4. Benjamin Tal and Emanuella Enenajor, "Degrees of Success: The Payoff to Higher Education in Canada," August 26, 2013, CIBC World Markets, *www.cibcwm.com. www.millenniumscholarships.ca/images/Publications/090623_POK1_backgrounder_EN.pdf.*

5. Tamar Lewin, "If Your Kids Are Awake, They're Probably Online," *New York Times*, January 20, 2010, *www.nytimes.com/2010/01/20/education/20wired.html?_r=0.*

6. Derek Thompson, "How Teenagers Spend Money," *The Atlantic*, April 12, 2013, *www.theatlantic.com/business/archive/2013/04/how-teenagers-spend-money/274949/.*

7. Judith Aquino, "Gen Y: The Next Generation of Spenders," *CRM*, February 2012, *www.destinationcrm.com/Articles/Editorial/Magazine-Features/Gen-Y-The-Next-Generation-of-Spenders-79884.aspx.*

Ann Marie Kerwin, "Millennials With Money? Find Out Where They Live and How They Spend," *Ad Age*, December 9, 2012, *http://adage.com/article/news/affluent-millennials-live-spend/238679/.*

8. "Digital Ad Spending Worldwide to Hit $137.53 Billion in 2014," eMarketer, April 3, 2014, *www.emarketer.com/Article/Digital-Ad-Spending-Worldwide-Hit-3613753-Billion-2014/1010736.*

9. S&P 500 Return Calculator, *http://dqydj.net/sp-500-return-calculator/.*

S&P 500 (^GSPC), *http://finance.yahoo.com/echarts?s=%5Egspc+interactive.*

10. *Ibid.*

11. *Ibid.*

Index